YOUR KINGDOM COME

Your Kingdom Come

by

C. LESLIE MITTON

WILLIAM B. EERDMANS PUBLISHING CO.
Grand Rapids, Michigan

© C. Leslie Mitton 1978
First published in the U.S.A. by
William B. Eerdmans Publishing Company
255 Jefferson, S.E., Grand Rapids, Michigan 49502

Library of Congress Cataloging in Publication Data

Mitton, C. Leslie.
    Your kingdom come.

    1. Kingdom of God—Biblical teaching.
I. Title.
BS2417.K5M53   231'.7   78-4542
ISBN 0-8028-1745-9

Printed in Great Britain

PREFACE

During my time as a tutor in a theological college my teaching was often concerned with the Kingdom of God in the teaching of Jesus. This present study, however, has enabled me to examine the subject with a new thoroughness, and especially to consider how writers in the New Testament, other than Jesus himself, have understood the Kingdom of God. I have been surprised to find how very little there is in the sayings of Jesus about the Kingdom to justify the common claim that for Jesus the coming of the Kingdom was an apocalyptic event associated with the coming of the Son of Man. I have also been impressed, contrary to my expectation, by the degree of wisdom shown by New Testament writers in their interpretation of the Kingdom.

I am grateful to Mr Richard Mulkern of Mowbrays for providing the stimulus to attempt this study of a subject very near to my heart.

Quotations from the Bible are usually taken from the Revised Standard Version, except where some special point makes a different rendering preferable.

C. L. MITTON

For
Helen,
Corinne
and
Diana
in gratitude

CONTENTS

I. INTRODUCTION

The Kingdom of God is the central theme of the proclamation of Jesus. It permeates all three of the synoptic gospels, occurring no fewer than 104 times. Of these instances ninety-one are found in sayings placed on the lips of Jesus (forty-six in Matthew, thirty-one in Luke and fourteen in Mark). Some of these are substantially the same saying which occurs in two or even three of these gospels. If allowance is made for these repetitions, there remain sixty-one entirely separate sayings of Jesus about the Kingdom of God.

This prominence of the phrase is the more striking because there is no precedent for it. It is very rare in the Old Testament, although God is there spoken of as a King who rules: 'Your God reigns' (Is. 52.7); 'Your Kingdom is an everlasting Kingdom' (Ps. 145.13); 'His Kingdom rules over all' (Ps. 103.19). Certainly the thought of God as the one true ruler pervades the Old Testament, but not the precise phrase 'the Kingdom of God'.

Nor does the phrase appear to have been particularly prominent in Judaism at the time of Jesus. Certainly there is a well-known prayer used in synagogue worship, perhaps as early as the first century, which asks that God will establish his Kingdom within the lifetime of those who pray; and the community at Qumran believed that God would establish his kingdom before long, after a time of suffering and bloodshed. One cannot, however, account for the centrality of the Kingdom of God in the teaching of Jesus by appealing either to the Old Testament or to contemporary Judaism.

Moreover it is not a feature which could have been read back into the time of Jesus by the post-resurrection Church. Although the phrase was remembered and occasionally appealed to as an honoured element in the tradition, after the

1

time of Jesus himself the phrase quickly dropped out of common use as an effective means of communicating the Gospel.

Its prominence therefore on the lips of Jesus in the synoptic gospels can be due only to the fact that he himself deliberately chose it and gave it emphasis and made it his own in a very special way, using it as a powerful medium for conveying the message he believed himself commissioned to proclaim. His constant use of it may be confidently accepted as one of the most firmly established facts about Jesus and his ministry. This indeed is conceded even by those scholars who in general show the greatest reluctance to acknowledge anything in the gospel record as undoubtedly historical.

Matthew, alone among the writers of the New Testament, presents us with a curious variation of the phrase. Apart from four exceptions, he consistently chooses to use the phrase 'the Kingdom of Heaven' instead of 'the Kingdom of God'. Both phrases, however, clearly carry the same meaning. 'Heaven' is introduced as a reverential synonym for 'God'. Most Jews felt a great reluctance to use the name of God if it could be avoided, lest they should be guilty of using it 'in vain' and so breaking the commandment. Where possible some roughly equivalent word was preferred as a substitute. Indeed many non-Jews feel something of the same reticence. A sensitive person may prefer to say: 'Heaven only knows', where someone less fastidious would bluntly say: 'God only knows'. Some scholars think that Jesus himself spoke of the Kingdom of Heaven and that Matthew is the only one who preserved the tradition accurately. Most, however, are inclined to think that Jesus spoke of the Kingdom of God and that Matthew (in all but four instances) preferred to use the less direct form of speech. Actually even the phrase 'the Kingdom of God', in the way Jesus used it, is itself a reverential device to avoid using a more immediate reference to God. What the phrase really means is 'God acting as King' or 'God in his sovereign power'. When Jesus speaks about the Kingdom of God he is in effect speaking about what happens when God begins to take charge of affairs.

The phrase 'the Kingdom of God', however, has become

much more than a first-century Palestinian concept which Jesus used in his teaching and which was later largely abandoned as the Church's mission became more and more involved with Gentiles. Because of the fact that Jesus had made such prominent use of it, and especially because it was incorporated in the prayer which his followers received from him, it has continued to be a regular part in the vocabulary of each new generation of Christians. All over the world, day by day, Christians still offer their prayer to God, as Jesus taught them: 'Your Kingdom come'.

For us today, however, living in the western world and in the twentieth century 'the Kingdom of God' is not at all a natural phrase to use. The word 'kingdom' has an archaic sound. At the time of Jesus, however, this was not the case. Most countries were then ruled by a king, or someone equivalent to a king, even if locally he may have been known as pharoah or tetrarch. Moreover at that time the king was one who actually ruled, one whom his subjects were required to obey. But today in the West there are very few kings, and those who still bear the name no longer exercise real power. They are kings only so long as they do not offend or oppose the wishes of those they are said to 'rule'. They are constitutional monarchs, and present to us a figure very different from the 'king' at the time of Jesus. The meaning, therefore, of the word 'king' today, so far from helping us to understand what 'king' meant then, can be a positive hindrance. A real king then was one who commanded and who was obeyed. This was true of a good king no less than of a wicked one. His 'goodness' consisted not in amiable indulgence towards insubordination, but in the actual fact that his commands when obeyed brought happiness, welfare and prosperity to his subjects as a whole. Modern ideas of kingship, therefore, do not help us to understand what was meant in the first century when God was spoken of as a king.

Another difficulty for us lies in the word 'kingdom'. The Hebrew word suggested the king's rule, wherever that rule was exercised, but for modern readers the word has come to mean the geographical area over which he rules. If we speak of the kingdom of Denmark, we mean a precisely definable territory

3

to the east of the North Sea. This localised meaning of the word creates another difficulty for us in understanding what is meant in the Bible by the Kingdom of God. This means the rule of God, a rule unlimited by any boundaries, and not at all a restricted area. Unfortunately there does not seem to be any single word in English which conveys accurately the meaning of the word as Jesus used it. 'Rule' or 'reign' are today commonly preferred to 'kingdom'. God's 'government' has recently been suggested. This is perhaps as good as any proposed variant, but even this sounds more static than was implied in the original word for 'kingdom'.

What we must all the time try to remember is that the phrase 'the Kingdom of God' is only a manner of speaking. There is actually no such entity as the kingdom. It is not a kind of establishment which God sets up. It is rather God himself exerting his rightful power to bring all people and all things under his control and to direct them by his will. It is God asserting his right to rule over human life and demonstrating his power to overthrow all powers hostile to his purposes and to subdue them to his will. When Jesus speaks of the Kingdom of God 'coming', he does not mean some 'thing' which is to appear, but God himself making his rule effective in the world of men. We have to remind ourselves constantly that in speaking of the kingdom we are speaking of something which has no existence at all apart from God himself. In a similar way also when we speak of the grace of God, or of his mercy or his love, we mislead ourselves if we allow ourselves to think of them as having some independent existence apart from God. They are merely verbal ways of referring to God himself as he acts graciously, mercifully, lovingly. So the Kingdom of God is a way of speaking of God himself as he acts with effective power for the welfare of his people.

The phrase 'the Kingdom of God' was one which Jesus chose to be a main vehicle of his message. Since our use of it today is entirely due to his emphasis on it, and since he taught his followers to pray for the coming of this kingdom, it is right that we should begin by trying to find out as accurately as possible what Jesus meant by it. Even if we are led ultimately to the conclusion that in the changed circumstances of today other expressions may well be more effective in conveying the same message to people of our time, its meaning for Jesus must be our starting point. This is all the more necessary because the phrase has often been used down the centuries and especially in the last century in ways very different from that intended by Jesus. Indeed it has tended to become a sort of universal symbol for human aspirations and ideals of widely different kinds. Whatever men at any one time have believed is the will of God for them and their society has been called 'the Kingdom of God', without any real attempt to ascertain whether it accords with what Jesus meant by it. So all kinds of human hopes have been somewhat carelessly, and sometimes very misleadingly, identified with God's Kingdom. Some of these have been oddly at variance with the teaching of Jesus and totally inconsistent with one another. Often they have been little more than temporary reflections of a passing social climate, or expressions of the personal preferences of the individual exponent.

Very commonly the Kingdom of God has been treated as an equivalent of 'heaven' or life beyond death. This appears in several hymns. 'He that into God's Kingdom comes must enter by this door' (the door being death). Indeed the phrase 'Kingdom-come' has become a kind of colloquial synonym for whatever lies beyond death. Others have identified the kingdom with the Church, the company of people among whom God's will prevails in the true obedience offered to him. But this is something which ought to be true rather than something which actually is. Some have equated it with what they regard as a God-ordained, established social order, in which each person 'knows his place' and meekly accepts it as part of the providence of God, whether that place involves the exercise of authority over others or submission to the authority of others. Others, again, have visualised the kingdom not in existing conditions, but in an ideal, just society to be striven for in the future, where no man shall be denied proper justice and inequalities will be removed, where men shall love their neighbours, all shall be secure from fear and want, and all will be given opportunity to fulfil their full human potential. Thought of in such terms the Kingdom of God has

5

been described as 'the universal moral community', 'the chief good of humanity' or even as 'the kingdom of self-respect'. Some have thought of the coming of the kingdom as a gradual process, a kind of moral evolution, while others prefer to use revolutionary terms with the implication that vigorous action by men in overthrowing unjust rulers will be the means by which God will achieve his righteous ends. Those of an apocalyptic turn of mind on the other hand see the kingdom as that which will supersede this present world order when God in some cosmic catastrophe sweeps it all away; for this 'new age' man can only wait and pray, for the action is wholly with God.

In view of this diversity of interpretations our primary aim must be to try to find out what Jesus himself meant by the kingdom, without reading into it our own unconscious presuppositions or the current hopes and ideals of our own environment. This, however, is not at all easy. In the first place it is difficult to separate what Jesus himself actually said from what the evangelists report him as saying. The historical facts about Jesus are no longer easily recoverable. Secondly it is perhaps impossible for anyone to approach this subject totally free from all personal preconceptions, preferences and prejudices.

Even among New Testament scholars of the highest rank, whose one aim has been to ascertain what Jesus himself meant by the Kingdom of God, there have been sharp differences of interpretation. The divergence is at its sharpest between those who are convinced that when Jesus spoke about the kingdom he spoke of a spiritual and moral force already active in his own ministry and destined to persist in the continuing life of the Christian community, and those, on the other hand, who insist that for Jesus the Kingdom of God was wholly in the future, expected as a catastrophic, apocalyptic event, perhaps very near but still to come. There is no doubt that there are sayings ascribed to Jesus which appear to give support to both sides of this controversy. Those who claim that for Jesus the kingdom was a present moral and spiritual force quote, for instance: (a) Mt. 12.28: 'If it is by the Spirit of God that I cast out demons, then the Kingdom of

6

God has come upon you'; and (b) Lk. 17.20,21: 'The Kingdom of God is not coming with signs to be observed, nor will they say, "Lo, here it is" or "There", for behold the Kingdom of God is in the midst of you' (or 'within you'). Those on the other hand who claim that for Jesus the Kingdom must be seen as something wholly in the future quote: (a) Mt. 16.18: 'There are some standing here who will not taste death before they see the Son of Man coming in his kingdom'; and (b) Lk. 22.18: 'I tell you that from now on I shall not drink of the fruit of the vine until the Kingdom of God comes'.

The argument between supporters of those two opposing interpretations has continued throughout the last hundred years and so far no agreed solution has been found. Great scholars like Harnack and Dodd support the first of the two options, and J. Weiss and A. Schweitzer the second. Harnack, of course, was aware of the apocalyptic sayings about the kingdom but interpreted them as just 'a manner of speaking', the use by Jesus of a contemporary fashion of speech in order to emphasise the vivid reality of the kingdom and of God's decisive part in its coming. The high-pitched language was, however, he argued, not meant to be taken literally. The apocalyptic phraseology was only the disposable 'shell'. It contained, but was not itself the essential message. Once the 'kernel' had been secured, the shell could be discarded. The 'kernel' consisted in those aspects of the teaching of Jesus which were strikingly original and at variance with commonly-held contemporary views, whether legalistic or apocalyptic. The essential 'kernel' was the reality of the Kingdom of God not as some future catastrophic event, but as 'the rule of God in the hearts of individuals'.

The protagonists on the other side of this dispute have pointed out the predominance of apocalyptic expectations in the gospels, not only in sayings about the kingdom, but also —perhaps especially—in sayings about the Son of Man. They have blamed their opponents for being wilfully blind to them, and totally failing to do justice to their presence and prominence in the gospels. They insisted that for Jesus the kingdom was wholly an apocalyptic concept, entirely in the future, even

7

though regarded as imminent. When asked how they harmonised their point of view with those sayings of Jesus which spoke of the kingdom as already present, they argue that when he spoke of it as already present it was only a kind of prophetic mannerism used in order to make vividly real both the absolute certainty of the coming of the kingdom and also its imminent nearness.

Modern scholars tend to support one or other of these two schools of thought. Those, however, who discount the apocalyptic element in favour of a present and moral interpretation are less inclined today to use the argument that this element was indeed used by Jesus but only as a 'shell' to contain the more important 'kernel'. Rather they contend that the apocalyptic elements in the sayings do not come from Jesus himself at all, but have been introduced into sayings of Jesus by the post-resurrection Church, which did in fact quickly become apocalyptic in its hopes and expectations. Leaders of the Church confidently predicted the early return of Jesus as Son of Man and began to identify this 'return' with the time of the establishment of God's Kingdom. It is clear from Paul's letters to the Thessalonians that at that time both Paul and his readers shared this expectation of a supernatural return of Christ in triumph. In consequence of this prevailing belief in the post-resurrection Church some of the sayings about the kingdom were adapted and rephrased to accord with this point of view. It was not done with any intention of distorting the truth or deceiving readers, but wholly with the aim of making explicit what the compilers of the gospels believed to be implicit in the sayings. This appears to be the view of the distinguished German scholar E. Käsemann, and his view is representative of that of many others. On the other hand there are modern scholars who believe that Weiss and Schweitzer were substantially correct, and that it was because Jesus himself spoke in apocalyptic terms that the early Church itself became apocalyptic in outlook. They argue that it is the non-apocalyptic elements in the gospels which must be seen as later modifications introduced by those who found apocalyptic hopes uncongenial.

It is true that the word 'apocalyptic' by derivation means

'that which reveals' but in common usage it has come to mean 'God revealing his power in some spectacular, supernatural action'. It is no longer used of quiet, recurring forms of revelation. Jesus saw God revealed in the simple beauty of the common wild flower and in the regularity of sunshine and showers which alone make fertility and growth possible. But the word 'apocalyptic' would not be applied to these unspectacular processes, but rather to such supernatural events as the Second Coming of Christ which in 1 Thess. 4.17 is associated with the sound of an archangel's voice and God's trumpet call; clouds will descend from heaven and Christ's people will be caught up in the clouds to meet the Lord in the air. Similarly the words of Mt. 24.30 would be described as apocalyptic: 'All people of the world ... will see the Son of Man coming on the clouds of heaven with great power and glory ... The angels will gather his chosen from the four winds, from the furthest bounds of heaven'. Among available descriptions of what 'apocalyptic' means we quote two which will guide us in our use of the word: firstly, apocalyptic is best understood to mean 'the sudden intervention of God in the affairs of the world to put all things right and bring history to end' (S. Neill in *The Interpretation of the New Testament*, p. 195). The second is from Schmithals in *The Apocalyptic Movement*: The apocalyptist 'no longer holds any hope for this eon, but places all his hope in a new eon beyond history'. When we ask if the 'apocalyptic' sayings in the gospels go back to Jesus himself, it is in this general sense that we shall interpret what is meant by 'apocalyptic'.

The word 'eschatological' has often—sometimes rather indiscriminately—been applied to the concept of the Kingdom of God. 'Eschatological' originally meant 'that which has to do with the end' but it has become a 'slippery', ambiguous word embracing a wide range of different meanings. It is better therefore to avoid its use unless its precise significance is made clear.

2. THE KINGDOM OF GOD IN THE TEACHING OF JESUS

To determine what the Kingdom of God meant for Jesus, we must turn to the synoptic gospels. In these three gospels, as we noted earlier, the phrase is used 104 times. Not all of these, however, occur on the lips of Jesus. Some appear in the questions of enquirers and others in general statements by the evangelists, as, for instance, when it is said that Jesus went into a certain area 'preaching the gospel of the Kingdom of God'. There are, however, ninety-one instances where the phrase appears in words attributed to Jesus. If duplicates are eliminated, we are left with sixty-one different sayings about the kingdom which are attributed to Jesus. Professor Jeremias analyses their sources as follows: Mark 13, 'Q' 9 (that is, the non-Markan sayings found in both Matthew and Luke), peculiar to Matthew 27, peculiar to Luke 12.

For those whose aim is to discover the authentic teaching of Jesus, however, not all of these sixty-one sayings carry equal weight. Some bear clear signs of editorial modification: either a reference to the kingdom has been introduced by the editor into a saying where it was not originally present, or the form of words about the kingdom has been changed as compared with an earlier version. It is difficult to be sure that any saying of Jesus is in exactly the same form as he spoke it, but we can at any rate make some progress towards our goal by eliminating those sayings which in their present form are clearly not wholly authentic.

Those which must be discounted on these grounds come mostly from Matthew. The mere number of sayings about the kingdom which he includes, in comparison with the other two, would tend to rouse suspicions. He reports forty-six, while Luke has thirty-one and Mark fourteen. When the actual instances in the Matthaean list are examined it is clear that in some of them a reference to the kingdom has been somewhat artificially inserted. For instance, Matthew introduces ten of the parables of Jesus with the words: 'The Kingdom of heaven is like ... (a merchant, a king, a net, etc.) and in some of these cases this particular form of introduction is quite inappropriate.

One does not doubt that Jesus did use some such introduction occasionally, nor does one doubt that many of his parables were associated with the kingdom. For instance, in Mk. 4.30 we read: 'Jesus said, How are we to liken the Kingdom of God, and in what comparison can we explain it? It is like a seed of mustard ...'. There is good reason for accepting this as a genuine word of Jesus. Two elements in it are characteristic of his teaching as a whole: the use of questions and the use of poetic parallelism (two sentences, balancing each other, each making the same point but in different words). Moreover in the parable of the seed of mustard the comparison between the seed and the kingdom is wholly appropriate. The mustard seed *is* like the kingdom in that it starts from something quite insignificant and yet quickly becomes astonishingly big. Four verses earlier, in Mk. 4.26, we also read: 'The Kingdom is as if a man should scatter seed ...'. Mark makes it clear that the comparison is not with the man himself, but rather with the whole action described in the parable—the sowing of the seed in the ground; its miraculous germination (without any human aid); its ultimate fruitfulness (in the presence of which the farmer is lost in wonder).

We need not doubt that Jesus did link the kingdom with parabolic teaching as Mark describes. But Matthew has taken an introductory formula, which is entirely appropriate at Mk. 4.30, and has used it inappropriately and artificially to introduce other parables in which there was originally no direct verbal reference to the kingdom. For instance, in Mt. 13.45 we read: 'The Kingdom of heaven is like a merchant seeking beautiful pearls ...' and in Mt. 18.23: 'The Kingdom of heaven is like a king ...' In fact, even if the parables are related to the kingdom, the parallel is not at all between the kingdom on the one hand and the merchant or the king on the other. The parallel is to be found at some other point in the story, and is concerned with the appropriate response of a man who finds himself confronted by the kingdom. This particular rather wooden formula which Matthew uses for introducing many of the parables is almost certainly a feature of Matthew's editorial work, and is not at all likely to come from Jesus himself. The eight instances in Matthew, therefore, where this formula is used by Matthew only (Mt. 13.24; 13.44; 13.45; 13.47; 18.23; 20.1; 22.2; 25.1) cannot be regarded as instances of the authentic words of Jesus, even though some of them may contain teaching about the kingdom.

There are also other words in Matthew ascribed to Jesus and which speak of the kingdom which must be treated with considerable reserve. These include those where Matthew is clearly reproducing a passage from Mark, but introduces significant changes into the wording. In some cases it is possible that he modified Mark to bring the saying nearer to the authentic word of Jesus. It is, however, in most cases much more likely that the modification is an attempt on Matthew's part to make the saying more appropriate to what Matthew thought Jesus intended to say, and reflects Matthew's work as a redactor rather than the original tradition of the words of Jesus. On three occasions, for instance, Matthew changes Mark's simple reference to Jesus as 'preaching' to the longer phrase 'preaching the gospel of the kingdom'. In Mk. 9.1 Jesus says that some of his hearers are going to live long enough to 'see the Kingdom of God come with power'. This section in Mark is reproduced in Matthew, but with a striking change of wording in this saying. What some of the eye-witnesses will live to see is described in Matthew 16.28, not as 'the Kingdom come with power', but as 'the Son of Man coming in his Kingdom'. This association of the coming of the Son of Man with the kingdom is in this passage at any rate the result of Matthew's handiwork and not an authentic word of Jesus. Again, at Mk. 10.37 James and John ask Jesus for privileged places near to Jesus 'in his glory'. In the parallel passage in Mt. 20.21, though Matthew for the most part reproduces Mark's wording, he makes two changes: he represents the request as coming from the mother of

James and John, and substitutes 'in your Kingdom' for Mark's 'in your glory'.

This observable tendency on the part of Matthew to make quite significant modifications in material which he is reproducing from Mark will make us suspicious in approaching the sayings where he differs from Luke in the so-called 'Q' material. Instances of this are (1) Mt. 6.10, where in the Lord's Prayer he adds to the Lucan petition 'Your Kingdom come' the further interpretative words: 'Your will be done' (cf. Lk. 11.2), and (2) Mt. 6.33 where Matthew enlarges Lk. 12.31, 'Seek the Kingdom of God' into 'Seek *first* his Kingdom *and his righteousness*'. One suspects that the additional material in Matthew is the work of Matthew the redactor.

In the reported sayings of Jesus about the kingdom which are peculiar to Matthew on the one hand and to Luke on the other, Luke has fifteen fewer references than Matthew, and this may suggest that he was less inclined than Matthew to introduce a reference to the kingdom into sayings which did not originally contain one. But this should not be taken for granted without scrutiny. At Lk. 21.31, for instance, he inserts a reference to the kingdom into a saying which appears in both Mark and Matthew without one. The Lucan version is therefore the one of the three which is most suspect.

By the use of tests like these a considerable number of the sayings about the kingdom attributed to Jesus can be eliminated from the first stage of our study. The presence of editorial modifications in them means that they cannot be relied on in their present form to reproduce the original teaching of Jesus. When these which are clearly open to some measure of suspicion are removed, there remain about twenty-five others which have a strong claim to authenticity. Without undue credulity we believe that these can be regarded as reflecting the mind of Jesus. It is this relatively small nucleus of sayings to which we first give our attention, and it is on them that we must primarily rely for reconstructing the meaning that the Kingdom of God had for Jesus.

We will briefly examine each of these, indicating those features in them which are significant for our purpose. At the end of the chapter we shall note those features which have kept on recurring in the different sayings. These will serve as a basis for determining what Jesus himself meant, when he spoke, as he so often did, about the Kingdom of God.

1. Mark 1.15:
The time is fulfilled and the Kingdom of God is at hand.

This is one of the sayings of Jesus about the Kingdom of God which is usually regarded as authentic. Mark has described the baptism of Jesus by John the Baptist, and his experience of temptation in the wilderness. Then, after the arrest of the Baptist, he is described as going into Galilee proclaiming the Gospel of God and saying: 'The time is fulfilled, and the Kingdom of God is at hand'. This declaration, 'The Kingdom of God is at hand' is also ascribed to Jesus elsewhere in the gospels. It is repeated in exactly the same words in Mt. 4.17 where Matthew is reproducing Mk. 1.15. Then Matthew puts the same words again on the lips of Jesus at 10.7, when Jesus at a later stage in his ministry is sending out the disciples on their missionary work and giving them instructions for their task. Luke also describes Jesus as using these words when he sends out disciples on missionary work (Lk. 10.9, 11), in a passage which has many verbal similarities with Matthew 10, and which therefore is usually regarded as derived from the non-Markan source which both Matthew and Luke used (often called 'Q'). The evidence therefore suggests that in both the primary sources, Mark and 'Q', this sentence was preserved as recalling an authentic memory of the message of Jesus. This agreement of two independent witnesses, both very early, points strongly to a reliable element in the tradition. Certainly it proves that the saying was embodied in the record of the teaching of Jesus from the earliest times.

Great controversy has raged over the precise meaning to be given to the Greek word here translated 'is at hand' (*ēngiken*). The simple Greek word from which it is formed (*engizō*) means 'draw near', but *ēngiken* is in the perfect tense of this verb. This is a significant tense in Greek for which we have no exact equivalent in English. It indicates an action which has taken place in the past, but which also has a continuing effect in the present. Here, if we laboured it, we could say that the perfect tense means: 'It has drawn near and is now very near'. It certainly means very much more than just an ordinary present tense which would be translated 'is drawing near'. The *New English Bible* seeks to do justice to this Greek perfect tense by translating it: 'The Kingdom of God is upon you'. Those who believe, as a result of their study of the gospels as a whole, that Jesus himself believed that the Kingdom of God was in some measure actually present in his ministry argue that this particular form of the verb could be translated: 'The Kingdom of God has arrived', that is, it is a present reality confronting human life now, and not just a future eventuality.

Those, however, who on other grounds are persuaded that for Jesus the kingdom lay wholly in the future insist that *ēngiken* does not mean 'has arrived', but only 'is near', 'is imminent'.

We leave for the moment the question whether the kingdom is here to be thought of as actually present or only as immediately imminent, and make a further point which is beyond doubt. The kingdom is here represented as *an advancing force*, a kind of relieving army coming to set free beleaguered prisoners. What has previously been understood as a promise to be fulfilled at some unspecified—even remote —date in the future is being put into immediate effect now. The relieving force has, as it were, already established a bridgehead in enemy-occupied territory, and from that foothold will soon be extending its liberating power over the whole area. God has begun to act. It may be your turn next to experience his salvation.

2. **Mark 4.31–32** (as also Mt. 13.31 and Lk. 13.18):
The Kingdom of God is like a grain of mustard seed, which when it is sown upon the ground is the smallest of all the seeds on earth: yet when it is sown it grows up and becomes the greatest of all the shrubs.

In Mark and Luke this brief parable is introduced by two questions, each of which in the style of Hebrew poetry expresses the same thought but puts it in different words:

With what can we compare the Kingdom of God,
Or what parable shall we use for it?

The use of questions and also the poetic parallelism are both characteristic features of the teaching method of Jesus. Another feature which confirms its authenticity is that what is here being taught is quite different from anything known to us in contemporary Judaism.

The mustard seed was regarded as quite peculiarly small even among such usually small things as seeds. Yet though it is so strikingly small the plant which quickly grows from it is remarkably large, far larger than other herbs or vegetables or flowers. Indeed it becomes like a small tree or shrub, in whose branches the birds find shelter. Some expositors have drawn from this parable the idea that Jesus spoke of the kingdom as something that grows slowly and imperceptibly, almost in an evolutionary process. But this is not the emphasis in the parable. Its point is rather that—like the mustard seed—from very small beginnings, in a very short space of time, the kingdom can assume large proportions. Unbelievably impressive results appear with astonishing speed. A tree takes years to grow; the mustard plant in only a few weeks is as big as some trees.

The parable therefore is stressing the *immense vitality* at work within the kingdom, the explosive energy released within it.

3. Mark 9.1:

Truly I say to you, there are some standing here who will not taste of death before they see the Kingdom of God come with power.

This saying has a very strong claim to be regarded as a genuine saying of Jesus. Both Luke (at 9.27) and Matthew (at 16.28) reproduce it, though each with some modification of wording. The introductory phrase is one which Jesus often used: 'Truly (that is, Amen) I say to you'. 'Amen' is an Aramaic word which Mark is content to represent in Greek letters without translating it into a corresponding Greek word. Matthew follows Mark in this, though Luke understandably replaces it with the normal Greek word for 'truly'. Another factor in favour of the saying's genuineness is that it could hardly have been invented by the post-resurrection Church, since for them it proved an awkward embarrassment, in that in the sense they gave to it the prediction was not fulfilled.

Matthew in 16.28 substantially reproduces Mark's words as far as the word 'see'; then he introduces a remarkable change of wording. Instead of 'the Kingdom of God come with power' he substitutes 'the Son of Man coming in his Kingdom'. Luke at 9.27 reproduces Mark's words in substance, but at the end omits the Markan words 'come with power', concluding with the words 'before they see the Kingdom of God'. Mark's words are clearly the original version of the saying which Matthew and Luke each altered slightly in his own way.

In the saying as Mark records it 'the coming of the Kingdom in power' is clearly an *event in the future*. It is not, however, expected in the immediate future since, by implication, some at any rate of the bystanders will have died. It is, however, not in the remote future, because some of them will live to witness it. Two significant phrases are used to describe this future coming of the kingdom. The first is the unexpected form of the word translated 'come' (literally it means 'having come'); and, second, it will have come 'with power'. The 'come' in this context could be translated as: 'They will see the Kingdom of God as a present reality'. The N.E.B. seeks to bring out the meaning of this participle by translating it as '*already come* with power'.

There are other sayings of Jesus (to be examined later) which speak of the kingdom as actually present in the ministry of Jesus. For instance, there are the words: 'If it is by the finger (or Spirit) of God that I cast out demons, then the Kingdom of God has come upon you' (Lk. 11.20; Mt. 12.28). His healing of human lives afflicted by illnesses which at that time in Palestine were ascribed to demon-possession was declared by Jesus to be evidence of the arrival of God's Kingdom. The healing was a clear sign that God was at work in their midst, triumphantly active through Jesus. So

17

for Jesus to say that some now present would live to see—later, but before long—the Kingdom of God coming would have added nothing of significance to what they had already experienced. What gives the promise its significance therefore is the new dimension which is promised—that the kingdom will have come *with power*. They have already seen the first signs of God's triumph in the restoration to full health of those afflicted human lives which Jesus healed during his ministry. What they will see within a generation is that small beginning greatly enhanced and multiplied. This would seem to be an appropriate description of the incredibly great expansion of Christian hope and healing which did take place within the period of a single generation. Through it far more lives were opened to the healing powers of God by the ever-widening Christian mission that had been possible within the actual ministry of Jesus, which in comparison had been so greatly constricted both in time and place.

The most natural meaning of this phrase, therefore, is to refer it to the enormous expansion of the Christian mission within, say, the lifetime of Peter, carrying forward God's purposes on an even larger scale than Jesus himself and his disciples had done in Palestine, as John 14.12 represents Jesus as promising will be the case: 'Greater works than these will he (the believer) do'.

It is clear, however, that Matthew (16.28) understood this 'coming of the Kingdom in power' as an apocalyptic event in the future when God would act with transcendent might and all human agencies would be swept aside—an overwhelming, supernatural event. What the survivors will live to see is 'the Son of Man coming (in Matthew *not*, as in Mark, "having come") in his Kingdom'. Matthew introduces the coming of the Son of Man into a context where originally Jesus had not used it; he also changes the Kingdom of God into the Kingdom of the Son of Man. The kingdom has faded into insignificance before what Matthew visualises as the glorious presence of the Son of Man and his coming. Matthew also changes Mark's perfect participle 'having come' into a present participle 'coming', as though the survivors will actually witness the arriving of the kingdom. This is surely an instance of early Christian interpretation being imposed on to a saying of Jesus which originally was quite different.

In the earliest form of the saying we notice again the use of the 'come' in relation to the kingdom. This Kingdom of God is one that 'comes'—once again like an *invading force*. In the time of Jesus it is already proving effective; at a later time, within a generation, its effectiveness will be greatly increased. A small beginning now will soon lead on to much greater consequences. There is an echo here of the expansion of the kingdom as visualised in the parable of the mustard seed.

4. Mark 10.14,15:

14. Let the little children come to me; Do not prevent them; For of such is the Kingdom of God.
15. Truly I tell you whoever does not receive the Kingdom of God as a little child, will not enter into it.

In the synoptic gospels there are two separate incidents involving Jesus and little children. The one (quoted above) in Mk. 10.14,15 tells how little children were brought to Jesus and the disciples tried to prevent them, and were rebuked by Jesus in two sayings, each of which contains a reference to the Kingdom of God.

Both Matthew and Luke reproduce verse 14, and Luke includes also verse 15. Matthew, however, does not use Mk. 10.15 in this context. Perhaps he feels, as some modern scholars do, that it does not really fit into this particular context very well. It is possible that verses 14 and 15 in Mk. 10 were originally independent sayings which Mark brings together because they both speak of the kingdom and of little children.

The second episode describing Jesus in contact with little children we need not consider here, since in the form given to it in Mk. 9.37 it does not include any reference to the kingdom. The disciples are arguing among themselves about which of them is 'greatest', and Jesus uses the presence of a little child to rebuke them. It is only in Matthew's development of Mark's story that the question (not very appropriately) becomes: 'Who is greatest *in the Kingdom of heaven*?' (Mt. 18.1).

This insertion of the kingdom by Matthew into a context where it does not occur in Mark is clearly an editorial modification. We will therefore at this point confine our attention to Mk. 10.14,15.

Mk. 10.14 asserts that childlikeness is a qualification for enabling someone to find a place in the Kingdom of God ('of such is the Kingdom'). But what aspect of childlikeness is intended? Mt. 18.3, though placed in a different context, may represent Matthew's understanding of the matter: 'Truly I tell you unless you turn and become as little children you will not enter the Kingdom of heaven'. Does this mean that as a child comes into the world by being born, so the disciples need a kind of re-birth to enter the world of the kingdom (as Jn. 3.3 makes explicit)? Certainly they need to 'turn' or, as A.V. had it, 'be converted'. N.E.B. translates the word as 'turn round' and T.E.V. as 'change'. The following verse in Matthew (Mt. 18.4), however, suggests a different understanding of 'childlikeness': 'Whoever humbles himself as this little child is greatest in the kingdom of heaven'. The conclusion of Jeremias, however, is that to 'become a child again' means to 'learn to say "Abba" again'. This would seem to imply an attitude towards God as father of dependence, obedience and affectionate trust. Certainly we should note that in these contexts the word used for 'children' means 'little children'. Indeed Luke makes the point even clearer by changing the word to 'babies'. We should probably think of two-year-old children rather than ten-year-olds.

Jeremias's suggestion is the best we know, but we have to concede that what Jesus meant by childlikeness in this context is no longer wholly clear. Perhaps we could note in support of Jeremias that in the Lord's Prayer the petition 'Your Kingdom come' is in fact addressed to one who is best known as 'Father'. The ruler in this kingdom is a father, and to know him as Abba, Father, is one of the keys to a place in his kingdom.

If Jeremias's suggestion illumines the meaning of Mk. 10.14, that still leaves us with Mk. 10.15 which is no less difficult to interpret with confidence. The Greek could mean either of two alternatives: either (a) 'Whoever does not receive the Kingdom of God as a child receives it ...'; or (b) 'Whoever does not receive the Kingdom as he receives a child ...'. It is, however, hardly likely in this context to be the second, although there are other sayings of Jesus about the importance of 'receiving a child' (Mk. 9.37; Mt. 18.5). If the first of the two translations is correct, then its meaning must be similar to that assigned to Mk. 10.14: the attitude of a happy child towards its father is the attitude towards God which characterises those who live in the kingdom.

The genuineness of this incident need not be questioned. This attitude of Jesus to little children is different both from that to be found in Judaism and also in the early Church. Moreover the second saying is introduced by the characteristic words of Jesus: 'Amen, I tell you ...'.

Though we may feel less than confident that we have accurately defined what is meant by 'childlikeness', we must bear it in mind and be on the alert to notice any clues in other sayings which may help us to understand it.

There are two words in Mk. 10.15, used in reference to the kingdom, which should be noted. They are 'receive' and 'enter'. Both these words emphasise an element of voluntary decision required of anyone who is to gain a place in the kingdom. Some sayings emphasise mainly God's initiative in the matter of the kingdom: the kingdom comes; it is a nucleus of explosive energy; it exercises pressure upon men and women. But on the other hand it is clear that the individual man or woman must be willing to 'receive' what God urgently offers, as a child accepts what his father provides. The words 'Whoever does not *receive*' implies that a man may refuse what is offered. This corresponds to the constant emphasis in the teaching of Jesus as a whole on *the need for a response of faith* if God's power is to become fully effective in a man's life. Similarly the word *enter* implies a decisive step, at least to the degree of accepting an invitation to 'come in'. Moreover this response is the response of an individual, not just the case of some anonymous member of a larger group acting on the command of a leader or through the decision of a majority vote. The word 'whoever' places the responsibility firmly on each person as a responsible individual.

21

5. Mark 9.47:

If your eye causes you to sin, pluck it out; it is better for you to enter the Kingdom of God with one eye than with two eyes to be thrown into Gehenna.

This reference to the Kingdom of God occurs in a threefold saying of Jesus in which he asserts that anyone wishing to discover the full benefits of a life consecrated to God must, if need be, be ready to sacrifice anything which may threaten to divide his loyalty to God—even though it may be something as precious as hand, foot or eye. Such threefoldness is a pattern of speech very frequently used by Jesus. The saying clearly emphasises that what may have be to sacrificed consists not only of evil things, but also of good things, if they prevent or distract a man from offering complete devotion to the will of God. Mark spells this out in three full parallel sayings: 'If your hand causes you to sin ...' 'If your foot causes you to sin ...', 'If your eye causes you to sin ...' Matthew in Mt. 18.8,9 understandably abbreviates. He combines foot and hand in one single saying, so that the whole unit becomes twofold rather than threefold. There is little doubt that Mark's version is nearer to the original form.

The main thrust of the saying is that nothing must be allowed to prevent a man from entering God's Kingdom. As with the treasure unearthed in a field, a man must be ready to dispose of everything else in order to gain it. Clearly the kingdom is not here thought of as some vast cataclysm which overtakes all mankind whether the individual wishes it or not. His entry depends on his own costly decision.

One point of special interest in this saying as Mark preserves it is that in the first two of the three parts of the saying the treasure to be gained as the result of sacrifice is described as *life*, but in the third part it is called 'the Kingdom of God'. There cannot be intended any real distinction of meaning. It is not that the sacrifice of an eye yields some privilege different from the sacrifice of hand or foot. It is merely that a synonym is introduced for the sake of variation. This can only mean that in some respects at any rate the Kingdom of God may be identified with what Jesus means by 'life'. Moreover this is not an isolated instance of the association of 'life' with the kingdom. It appears again, for instance, in Mk. 10. 23,25, which is the saying to be considered next.

In Mk. 9.43–47 the grim alternative to 'life' or 'the Kingdom' is called Gehenna (in R.S.V. 'hell'), the refuse dump outside Jerusalem where fires continually burned. Here it appears to be used as a symbol for rejection and destruction after death. We may assume therefore that 'life' and 'the Kingdom of God' in this context also imply some future dimension. Gehenna, however, is not a word with particularly apocalyptic associations. It can be used of the punishments in the after-life which follow an evil life in the ordinary way. However, the use of 'life' in the teaching of Jesus includes far more than life after death. For the fourth evangelist 'eternal life' is explicitly a quality of life into which the Christian may enter here and now; it can be a present reality as well as a future hope. So in the synoptics 'life' may be both a present privilege and a future one. For instance, in Lk. 12.15 Jesus speaks of a man's life as consisting of more than his material possessions.

Once again we notice the use of the word *enter* in relation to the kingdom, with its implication of a real element of personal responsibility.

6. Mark 10.23–25:

How hard it is for those who have riches to enter into the Kingdom of God. (24) Children, how hard it is to enter the Kingdom of God. (25) It is easier for a camel to go through the eye of a needle than for a rich man to enter the Kingdom of God.

These three sayings of Jesus may be regarded as authentic. Luke (18.24,25) takes them over from Mark more or less word for word, and Matthew 19.23,24 reproduces Mk. 10.23 and 25 (omitting verse 24), and, interestingly enough, retains here the phrase 'Kingdom of *God*' (Mt. 19.24) though in most other cases he changes it to Kingdom of *Heaven*. But the further ground for accepting the saying's authenticity (apart from the value Matthew and Luke attached to it by the mere fact of reproducing it) is that it is sharply at variance with the teaching of both traditional and contemporary Judaism, and also with the outlook of the early Church. Traditional Judaism regarded wealth as one of the blessings God conferred on the righteous. The incredulous attitude of the early Christian probably found expression in the exasperated comment attributed to Peter in Mk. 10.26: 'Who then can be saved?' Moreover the difficulties which early Christians found in this saying are reflected in several textual variants which found their way into the later manuscripts. For instance, some of them introduced into verse 24 the added phrase, 'those who trust in riches', thus transferring the hindrance from the mere possession of wealth to the possessor's over-reliance on it. This significant modification of what Jesus actually said has indeed remained the official attitude of the Church on this sensitive issue, even though it is clearly a device for evading the stark reality of the plain words of Jesus. Most modern translations omit this added phrase, recognising it as an obvious attempt by some later copyist to soften the hard teaching of Jesus, or (as R.S.V. and N.E.B. do) relegate it to a footnote. The offence in the original saying is a guarantee of its genuineness.

It is true that (in verse 23) Jesus says merely that it is hard for those who have riches to enter the kingdom—hard, but not impossible. But verse 25 with its picturesque comparison with a camel's futile struggle to get through a needle's eye implies that it is quite impossible—though allowance should be made for humorous exaggeration which Jesus often used to make his teaching memorable. In addition the contortions of commentators as they attempt to soften the severity of verse 25 show again how offensive this saying of Jesus has proved. But all attempts to represent the needle's eye as a small gate in a city wall or to make a change in only one letter so that the camel may be turned into a rope have proved to be only imaginative guesses with no foundation in fact. All this evidence of embarrassment serves to confirm the authenticity of the original sayings.

In Mark 10.14,15 Jesus commended childlikeness as a qualification for the kingdom. Here wealth and the human characteristics it fosters are declared to be disqualifications. This suggests that one saying may help in the interpretation

24

of the other, one being perhaps the opposite of the other. Is it that wealth tends to make a man self-sufficient and independent of God and arrogant and presumptuous towards others in that he learns to assume that money will purchase for him any special privilege he wants? Is it that he is trapped in a mesh of values in that everything has its cash-value attached to it? In contrast childlikeness implies a recognition of one's dependence on our Father, the Father's right to obedience, a freedom from the social tyranny which measures all things in terms of money. In this connection we recall the first beatitude which pronounces the poor 'blessed' (Lk. 6.20) because theirs is the Kingdom of God. We notice that in each of these three sayings the phrase '*enter* the kingdom' occurs with its implication of the moral *responsibility* which each man must bear in the action he takes.

These sayings about riches in Mark 10 follow on immediately after the incident of the rich young ruler. It is therefore not without significance that the rich man's question as he came to Jesus was: 'What must I do to inherit eternal *life*?' The comment of Jesus on his refusal to pay the price speaks of the difficulty of a rich man finding entrance into the *Kingdom*. Life and Kingdom are here, as in Mk. 9.42–47, treated as equivalent to each other. It may sound as though 'eternal life' is here to be understood as future life; and yet it is clear that the young man was painfully aware that though he had kept all the rules it was something *in the present* which he lacked and knew he lacked, some quality of life he felt full obedience to God should bring into being here and now. This saying provides another difficulty for those who argue that for Jesus 'life' and the 'kingdom' were concepts belonging entirely to the future.

7. Mark 14.25:

Truly I say to you, I shall not drink again of the fruit of the vine until that day when I drink it new in the Kingdom of God.

Matthew in 26.29 substantially repeats these words, though he changes 'Kingdom of God' to 'Kingdom of my Father'. Luke 22.18 has a very similar saying, though scholars differ in their opinions as to whether Luke has derived the saying from Mark and re-phrased it, or whether he received it from a separate source wholly independent of Mark. His version is:

> I tell you that from now on I shall not drink of the fruit of the vine until the Kingdom of God comes.

Mark's form of the saying probably has a stronger claim to authenticity, since Luke's version shows signs of having been assimilated to other sayings about the kingdom. Mk. 14.25 contains several semitisms, and this fact indicates at any rate an early origin for the saying. The word translated 'truly' (as in Mk. 9.1 and 10.15) is actually '*amēn*' (a Hebrew word merely transliterated into Greek letters); the 'fruit of the vine' (meaning wine) has a semitic sound, and so too has the phrase 'until that day'. The saying also begins with the phrase characteristic of many emphatic sayings of Jesus: 'Truly I say to you'.

The words were spoken by Jesus during the Last Supper when he knew that his enemies had reached the decision to bring about his early death. It declares that this will be his last formal meal on earth. Some have argued that it is more than just a recognition of a grim fact, and that it is in fact a form of Nazirite vow renouncing strong drink until a certain course of action is complete. This, however, seems to read too much into the words.

Some believe that the form of the saying indicates that Jesus expected the coming of God's Kingdom in some dramatic form at the time of his death. Luke's version may be interpreted in this way, but there is no suggestion of this in Mark's form of the saying. It does, however, clearly have a future reference to something that lies beyond his own death. Beyond his death he will be within God's Kingdom. The kingdom is already a present reality beyond this earthly sphere. Even if it has begun to break through into the world of men, that is still only a small beginning. A much greater fulness of its coming lies ahead. If we ask: 'Where is that kingdom now for whose coming to this earth Christians are taught to pray?', we reply, 'It is where God is King'. There is a sense in which God rules eternally, even if on earth his authority is defied. His Kingdom in that sense is an eternal kingdom. From its being in eternity that kingdom is thrusting itself into time. When Jesus speaks of drinking wine 'new' in the Kingdom of God, does he mean that beyond his human death he will be received into that eternal kingdom, that kingdom which is coming and will come later with power on to the earth? Or does he mean that before he needs to drink again that kingdom will have been established with apocalyptic splendour and suddenness here on earth?

If Jesus expected the kingdom to be established on earth by some imminent apocalyptic event, then presumably he was mistaken (as he was if Matthew 16.28 is accepted as genuine, in spite of its variation from the corresponding verse in Mark). That event did not take place as expected. But here in Mark there is no reference to the *coming* of the kingdom on earth. That element belongs to Luke's re-phrasing of the saying. If the Markan saying stood by itself (apart from the other apocalyptic sayings in the gospels) the most natural meaning for it to carry here would be that Jesus sees death so near that for him his next proper meal, as it were, will be the heavenly *banquet* in God's Kingdom in Heaven.

Jesus appears to expect confidently that he will be sharing in such a celebration banquet in God's Kingdom immediately beyond his expected death. There is no hint of that other contemporary belief that the body would lie in the ground till the final resurrection and the day of judgement. There is to be immediate participation in life with God, not dissimilar from the promise which Luke describes Jesus as making to the dying thief: 'Today you will be with me in paradise'.

These seven sayings about the kingdom, which Mark ascribes to Jesus (1 to 7) are free from elements which make it difficult to assign them with some confidence to Jesus. There are no strong reasons for regarding them as inauthentic, and indeed in most cases good grounds for treating them as accurate reflections of words of Jesus. There are, however, two other similar sayings in Mark, which we should take notice of at this point, even if we have to conclude that their authenticity is more open to question. They are Mk. 12.34 and Mk. 4.11.

8. Mark 12.34:

You are not far from the Kingdom of God.

Jesus addresses these words to an enquirer who has shown real discernment concerning the importance of the two great commandments in the Law. The main ground of doubt about their authenticity is that Matthew and Luke, though they both report this incident from Mark omit these words spoken by Jesus to the enquirer. In other Markan sayings we have regarded the adoption of the saying by Matthew and Luke as supporting evidence of its reliability. The absence of such support, therefore raises a query.

Apart from Matthew's and Luke's omission of the saying, the words themselves have a strong claim to authenticity, because they reveal a certain independence of thought. They are not just a repetition of other sayings or of customary attitudes. They do not sound like the words an early Christian might have invented. The kingdom, in this saying, is not something wholly in the future. It is near and available, and a man's nearness to it is partly determined by his own moral attitude and spiritual insight. The words can hardly mean that the man is in a frame of mind to welcome the kingdom when it bursts in upon him at some future date. Rather his understanding that love for God and neighbour is far more important than the multitude of other rules among which they are found, and that such love matters far more than the meticulous observance of a multitude of regulations about ritual practices has brought him part of the way that leads to the kingdom.

Here then we find emphases which we have already seen to be characteristic of Jesus: that the kingdom is in some measure *present*, and that the key to entering it lies in part in the ability of the person concerned to bring the right attitude of mind—a *proper response*.

9. Mark 4.11:

To you has been given the secret (mystery) of the Kingdom but for those outside everything is in parables, so that they may see but not perceive....

Mt. 13.11 and Lk. 8.10 both reproduce the substance of

Mk. 4.11. There is little doubt that these words represent Mark's own understanding of the teaching of Jesus to the disciples and to the crowds. The whole passage seems to be part of Mark's attempt to construct his own theory about the parables. It is quite incredible that Jesus spoke his parables with the purpose of deceiving or bewildering his hearers. It is moreover unlikely that Jesus ever spoke of 'the mystery' of the kingdom or associated it with the difficulties presented by the parables. These modes of thinking and the use of the word 'mystery' belong rather to the post-resurrection Church.

If the phrase 'the mystery of the kingdom' goes back to Jesus it would mean (not the difficulty of relating the parables to the essential message he proclaimed) but the fact that his teaching about the kingdom was so different from what was customary that many people found it extremely 'puzzling', since its acceptance meant discarding familiar ideas and trying to come to terms with a disconcertingly new point of view.

We do not, however, believe that this saying is sufficiently free from suspicious elements to use it to reconstruct the thought of Jesus about the kingdom.

We have considered nine sayings of Jesus about the kingdom recorded in Mark's gospel, seven or eight show no evident sign of editorial revision and may be taken as reflecting the mind of Jesus himself. We now turn to a second group of sayings about the kingdom. These are the ones which do not occur in Mark, but are found in both Matthew and Luke. Both Matthew and Luke must have found these sayings in a common area of tradition, to which each independently had access. This source has in common parlance has been called 'Q', though the use of a single symbol should not create the assumption that 'Q' was necessarily a single document.

10. Mt. 5.3 and Lk. 6.20:

Blessed are the poor in spirit for theirs is the kingdom of heaven (Mt. 5.3).
Blessed are you poor, for yours is the kingdom of God (Lk. 6.20).

In both Matthew and Luke this saying stands as the first beatitude. The two versions are not quite identical. Matthew spiritualises the meaning of the word 'poor', and makes the sayings more general by speaking of 'the poor' rather than 'you poor'. Matthew applies the blessing to all the poor; Luke applies it to those addressed (probably the disciples) who may count themselves 'blessed' in spite of their being 'poor'. Luke's group of beatitudes in this context contains only four, whereas Matthew's has eight. These include all Luke's four plus four others. However we may judge these extra four, there is good reason to think that the four which are common to both Matthew and Luke reflect the teaching of Jesus himself.

This one speaks of the Kingdom of God as a great *privilege* for those who possess it, and therefore a treasure to be coveted. Those who possess it are described as 'blessed'; they are to be congratulated. Moreover this great privilege is available to those who are 'poor'. We noted in our consideration of Mk. 10.14,15 (§4) that childlikeness is a quality which enables people to receive the kingdom. What is meant here by being 'poor' is something not dissimilar—an absence of self-importance, freedom from the domination of standards of value imposed by society and from personal involvement in greed for wealth and status and worldly privilege. It is the opposite of the attitude engendered by wealth, which (as is taught in Mk. 10. 23–25, section 6) excludes men from the kingdom.

In Luke the second and third beatitudes which follow are attached to a promised reward in the future tense: the hungry *shall* be satisfied and those who weep *shall* laugh. Also in the summarising verse which follows (Lk. 6.23) the promised reward is spoken of as being 'great' and 'in heaven'. Heaven, however, in this context does not necessarily mean 'life after death'. It could be a reverential synonym for God himself. In this sense the saying would mean that though the Christian life may well lead to lack of wealth, security, comfort and popularity, it does make men 'rich toward God' (to borrow a phrase from Lk. 12.2), whether now or hereafter. The future tenses of the verbs do, however, seem to refer to something beyond this life, though this cannot be proved. In that case they could refer either to life with God in heaven or to some apocalyptic future following a cataclysmic in-breaking of God's rule upon the earth.

In the first beatitude, however, there is no future reference at all. Both Matthew and Luke specifically insert the present tense of the verb 'is'. In contrast to the future tenses in other beatitudes this seems to be a quite deliberate insistence on the importance of the present tense. Disciples may here and now live in the kingdom. This particular privilege is not something which has to be waited for in some indeterminate future.

It is interesting that, in Matthew, of the eight beatitudes six have their promise relating to the future. The two which have present tenses are the first and the eighth, and in each of these two cases the assurance is: 'Theirs *is* the Kingdom of heaven'.

11. Mt. 6.10 and Lk. 11.2:

Thy Kingdom come, thy will be done,
   On earth as it is in heaven (Mt. 6.10).
Thy Kingdom come (Lk. 11.2).

Both Matthew and Luke include the prayer which Jesus is reported as giving to his disciples. Luke's version is the shorter, and most scholars are inclined to think that it is this shorter version which lies nearer to the actual words of Jesus. Both versions include the petition: 'Your Kingdom come', and express it in exactly the same words. Matthew, however, adds a parallel sentence: 'Your will be done, on earth as it is in heaven'. Matthew probably understood these words, not as an additional petition, but as an alternative way of asking for the same thing. For him the prayer, 'Your Kingdom come' could equally well be expressed as: 'Your will be done', since where God's kingdom is there God's will prevails.

It is more than likely, however, that the way Matthew's additional phrase has been traditionally translated and understood has fostered a way of thinking of God's Kingdom which neither Jesus nor Matthew intended. The Greek words which Matthew actually used are misleadingly misrepresented in the conventional translation. Nor do all modern translations correct the error. The familiar rendering: 'Thy (or "Your")

31

will be done' can all too easily give the impression that it is when men *do* God's will that God's Kingdom comes—as though the coming of the kingdom is identical with human morality. But this emphasis is not present in the words used by Matthew. What his words actually mean is: 'May God's will prevail' or 'be established', with a complete absence of any emphasis on man's part in it. The emphasis is wholly on what God does, and man's part is to accept and fall in line with what God is doing. The coming of the kingdom is what God does, and when his kingdom is at work within us our lives may serve his purposes—as Paul put it in Philp. 2.13, 'God is at work in you both to will and to work for his good pleasure'. The careless phrase about man's 'building the Kingdom of God' which has been popularly accepted in this century and has even found its way into modern hymns, may have been partly fostered by this misleading translation of Mt. 6.10b. But Matthew's words themselves leave all the initiative with God ('May your will prevail') as it was in the original teaching of Jesus. Probably, however, the petition 'Your Kingdom come' is from Jesus himself, and the added words in Matthew from the church in which and for which Matthew wrote.

The original nucleus of this saying may confidently be treated as an authentic word of Jesus: 'Your Kingdom *come*'. Here again we find the emphasis on the 'coming' of the kingdom. It is an insurgent force, a vital, powerful energy moving in upon the world of men. The Christian prays that this divine energy will overcome all that seeks to thwart it and establish itself powerfully in human hearts and society.

We note also the association of the idea of God as *Father* with the somewhat different idea of his kingdom. This prayer is addressed, in both Matthew and Luke, to 'Father', and it is the Father's Kingdom for whose coming we pray. A Father's Kingdom is his family. This association of the Kingdom of God and the thought of God as Father will be noted again in other sayings of Jesus.

Seek first his Kingdom and his righteousness and all these things shall be yours as well (Mt. 6.33).

Seek his Kingdom and these things shall be yours as well (Lk. 12.31).

One long unit of the teaching of Jesus has been preserved in almost identical wording in Mt. 6.25–33 and Lk. 12.22–31. This is the passage where Jesus remonstrates with people who live lives consumed with anxiety about what they are going to eat and drink and wear. They are told to watch the birds and flowers and learn from their example. The birds are carefree and the flowers serene; they do not wear themselves out by worry over fine food or splendid clothes. The secret of this freedom from anxiety, says Jesus, lies in the awareness that your Father knows all about your needs of food and clothes, and can be trusted to provide what is sufficient. Therefore 'seek his kingdom and these other things will be yours as well'. That is how Lk. 12.31 records the saying. Matthew's version, by introducing small additions, both changes the emphasis and seeks to clarify the meaning. The changed emphasis is found in the command to seek *first* the kingdom, and in the promise that '*all* these things' will be yours as well. The explanatory word is 'righteousness', added apparently to suggest in practical terms what the significance of the kingdom is—'seek first his Kingdom *and his righteousness*'. The introduction of this word 'righteousness' to interpret the meaning of kingdom recalls how in the Lord's Prayer Matthew suggests that 'Your Kingdom come' may be understood to mean: 'Your will prevail'. To live in God's Kingdom means to live in obedience to the will of the King, and for Matthew the will of God is righteousness.

Once again we notice here the association of the thought of God as *Father* with the idea of the kingdom. It is because 'your Father knows that you need these things' that you are bidden to 'seek his Kingdom'. The command to '*seek*' is also a word which implies moral response and endeavour. It is more than just waiting passively for some overwhelming event looked for in the future. The summons is to make our gaining of the Kingdom our most determined purpose in life—to identify our purpose with God's.

Clearly, however, this saying of Jesus means that when man's dominating purpose is to let God rule his life, worry about food and clothes (and maintaining the social conventions in regard to them) is excluded by other concerns.

There is clearly a link between this saying and others we have already considered: for instance, the blessing pronounced on the '*poor*' (who have no position they must try to keep up) and the woe upon the rich, with their almost inescapable pre-occupation with status and appearances, a concern which makes it specially hard to seek first God's Kingdom.

13. Mt. 8.11–12:

Many will come from east and west and sit at table with Abraham, Isaac and Jacob in the kingdom of heaven, while the sons of the Kingdom will be thrown into outer darkness.

Lk. 13.28–29:

You will weep and gnash your teeth when you see Abraham and Isaac and Jacob and all the prophets in the Kingdom of God and you yourselves thrust out. 29. And men will come from east and west and north and south and sit at table in the Kingdom of God.

This saying appears in both Matthew and Luke, but in entirely different contexts and with the phrases arranged in a different order. The variations in the two sayings may be partly accounted for by the attempt of each evangelist to adapt the saying to the context in which he places it. Since neither context is wholly convincing it is best to regard the saying as, prior to Matthew and Luke, an independent unit which in the tradition at an earlier stage had been remembered without any context. The gist of the saying is clear: Jesus declares that in God's Kingdom Jews cannot rely on receiving an automatic place merely because they are Jews; some will indeed be excluded, and foreigners will be received in their place alongside the great figures of the Jewish past. Jesus when he spoke these words probably found himself confronted by Jews who thought that Jews had a kind of monopoly of God and that therefore God's Kingdom was wholly reserved for them. They thought of themselves as 'sons of the Kingdom'. Jesus, however, insists that Jews have no such prerogative in the kingdom. It is not membership of one particular nation (or social group) but a man's personal response to God as Father which is the qualification for life in the kingdom—and this is *open to all men* whether Jews or not. Here we find again the idea of a celebrating *banquet* in the kingdom—a conventional symbol of *joy*.

Some may wish to deny that Jesus so clearly visualised the inclusion of non-Jews in the Kingdom, and may quote in support of their dissent such words of Jesus as are recorded in Mt. 15.24: 'I was not sent except to the lost sheep of the house of Israel'. But this saying did not mean that Jesus's concern was limited to those of his own Jewish race. The emphasis in the saying is wholly on the word 'lost': his concern was for those who had become outcasts of society—primarily no doubt the taxgatherers and sinners—rather than for those already counted as 'righteous'.

The saying, therefore, in its most reliable nucleus, implies that God's Kingdom is a *universal* kingdom, open to all men and women of all nations on the same conditions, not the prerogative of a privileged few. It is 'catholic' in the best sense of the word—all-inclusive.

Support for the genuineness of the saying comes from the fact that it is utterly at variance with contemporary Jewish thinking. It is true that it could have been invented within that part of the Church which later supported the Gentile mission, but the wording is extremely Jewish and certainly suggests a Jewish rather than a Hellenistic origin.

14. Mt. 11.11b and Lk. 7.28b:

Among those born of women none is greater than John; yet he who is least in the Kingdom of God is greater than he.

Some scholars have felt that the second part of this verse is most inappropriate following as it does immediately after a very great tribute paid to John the Baptist, to the effect that of all human beings of the past none is greater than he. The immediate qualification of this high praise (by the assertion of the superiority of even the humblest Christian) may conceivably have developed in some area of Christian work where followers of the Baptist continued successfully as an independent sect in rivalry to the Christian Church. In so far as it can be relied on as a true reflection of genuine words of Jesus it is clearly a most emphatic statement that what has begun with Jesus (with his proclamation of the coming of the Kingdom) is something *radically new*, which supersedes even the very best from the past. It also speaks of the Kingdom as something *present* rather than merely in the future.

15. Mt. 11.12:

From the days of John the Baptist until now the Kingdom of heaven has suffered violence (*biazetai*) and men of violence take it by force.

Lk. 16.16:

The law and the prophets were until John; since then the good news of the Kingdom of God is preached and every one enters it violently (*biazetai*).

This saying, reported very differently by Matthew and Luke, is of fascinating interest, because it clearly preserves something striking and original in the teaching of Jesus. Unhappily we cannot base any conclusions on it because both the particular wording of the original saying and the meaning of it are so uncertain. The source both of its fascination and of the problem it poses lies in the use in each form of the saying of an unusual Greek word. This is *biazetai*, which is derived from a Greek verb (*biazō*) meaning 'violate'. Part of the difficulty is that in Matthew 'the Kingdom' is the subject of this verb, whereas in Luke the subject is 'everyone'. The major difficulty, however, is that this form of the Greek word can be translated in seemingly almost opposite ways, either with an active or a passive meaning. That is, it could mean either 'is violently active' or 'is suffering violence'.

Perhaps the only convincing conclusion which can be drawn is that here the Kingdom of God is recognised (in both forms of the saying) as something already *present*, something that

36

exceeds what John the Baptist had stood for. The kingdom is either actively at work or is being actively challenged; but in either case it is a present reality, not a future expectation.

Perhaps we could also add that some action of a vigorous and forceful nature is involved: either the kingdom itself is regarded as thrustful, or those who enter it (or oppose it) are thrustful and aggressive. There are parallels to both these aspects in the rest of the teaching of Jesus.

15. Mt. 12.28 and Lk. 11.20:

If it is by the Spirit (or 'finger' in Lk. 11.20) of God that I cast out demons, then the Kingdom of God has come upon you.

This saying appears in almost identical form in both Matthew and Luke, and also in exactly the same context. The one variation of wording is that Matthew has 'spirit of God' and Luke has 'finger of God', but both alternatives really mean the same. It is God's action in and through Jesus which is declared to be the effective force in the healing work of Jesus. Whether it is 'Spirit of God' or 'finger of God' the emphasis is the same—on what God himself has done. Jesus does not see his healing work as the expression of some personal accomplishment of his own. He is merely the channel, or at most the agent, through whom this invading power from God is working effectively in human life.

Jesus is insisting that his own ability to cast out demons is simply an indication that God's power is operating through him. At that time there was in Palestine a general belief in demons. They were understood to be the cause of many ills which plagued and crippled human life. Particularly if an illness had a strong emotional content and some uncontrollable, compulsive element in it, it was ascribed to the presence and domination of an evil spirit. There is no doubt that Jesus possessed a remarkable power to bring a sense of release and freedom to such sufferers. This Jesus declared to be God's doing. God had come to the possessed life and set it free. He had driven out the evil thing. This, said Jesus, is what is meant by the coming of God's Kingdom into human life. God takes control, instead of the evil things which had wrongfully seized power.

There are very few scholars who would question the authenticity of this particular saying. Certainly its origin is earlier than Matthew's gospel, because he surprisingly retains here the phrase 'Kingdom of *God*' instead of using 'Kingdom of heaven' as he does on almost every other occasion. It must have come to him in that form. The saying unquestionably asserts the *present* reality of the Kingdom. Jesus speaks of what has already happened as evidence of the commanding presence of the kingdom. Not only is the kingdom present, but it is present as something which is effectively *active*. There is forcefulness in it.

We note too that the kingdom can not only break strong resistance and overcome powerful opposition, but also that what it achieves is wholly for the restoration and *healing* of human life, enabling it to rise above disablement and become its own best self.

17. Mt. 13.33:

The Kingdom of heaven is like leaven which a woman took and hid in three measures of meal till it was all leavened.

Lk. 13.20,21:

To what shall I compare the Kingdom of God? It is like leaven which a woman took and hid in three measures of meal till it was all leavened.

Matthew introduces this parabolic saying with the formula he has adopted for introducing many of his recorded parables: 'The Kingdom of heaven is like ...'. Luke, however, introduces the parable by using a question, as Mark does for the parable of the mustard seed (Mk. 4.30). Such a question is very characteristic of the teaching method of Jesus, and it is most probable that Luke in this case has retained the form which the unit had in the tradition before Matthew and Luke took it over. The parable is indeed a close parallel—a kind of 'twin'—to that of the mustard seed, and both Matthew and Luke recognise this by placing them next to each other in their gospels. Both parables speak of the kingdom as possessing an inner *vital energy*, which enables it, though starting from a very small beginning, to achieve a great result in a comparatively short time.

The seventeen sayings so far considered are those which have multiple attestation. They include those from Mark which are reproduced in either Matthew or Luke or in both, and those which, though absent from Mark, are used by both Matthew and Luke and appear to come from some common stream of tradition which ante-dates both Matthew and Luke.

There remain others which are found in only one of the gospels—either Matthew or Luke. The fact of there being only one witness means that more than usual caution must be taken before accepting such a saying as authentic. Certainly if such a saying carries features which are recognisably the peculiarity of the evangelist who reports it we shall have to treat its authenticity with suspicion. If, however, the saying seems to be free from editorial modification, and especially if in some respect it even runs counter to what elsewhere can be shown to be the normal preference of the editor, then it merits close attention. A further claim to authenticity must be conceded if the saying, while differing from current Judaism and perhaps even from the usual emphases of the early Church, shows marked congruence with the main body of the teaching of Jesus—without just repeating mechanically identical verbal phrases.

Luke has four such sayings. Though they occur only in Luke, they all have a strong claim to be regarded as authentic.

18. Lk. 9.62:

No one who puts his hand to the plough and looks back (N.E.B. 'keeps looking back') is fit for the Kingdom of God.

The failing which is rebuked is not one brief backward glance in a passing moment of discouragement, but a continuing attitude of regret for what has been left behind and a persistent doubt about the wisdom of the decision which has been taken. The kind of disciple whom God needs in his work for the kingdom is one who has committed himself with such decisiveness that he no longer even considers the question whether or not it was the right decision. The full cost has been counted. A decisive step has been taken. The commitment which has been made is total and for life.

A metaphor from the handling of a plough is entirely in character with what we know of Jesus. The emphasis on the need for decisiveness and total commitment is also a recurring theme in his teaching. We may therefore with some confidence include this saying in the authentic teaching of Jesus about the kingdom. It is wholly in line with other parts of his teaching, with its emphasis on the need for total and continuous *commitment* and the freedom from the crippling effects which recurring doubt and questioning create (cf. 1 Cor. 10.9–11. Here once again is the implication that though the Kingdom is God's act and achievement, it is not action of a kind which overrules human decision but waits upon it and acts through it. The kingdom can be furthered by man's total, unquestioning obedience to God and can be hindered by vacillation and hesitation.

20. Lk. 12.32:

Fear not, little flock, for it is your Father's good pleasure to give you the Kingdom.

There is nothing in this saying which is obviously due to editorial revision. 'Fear not' is a phrase found on the lips of Jesus in both Mark and Matthew as well as Luke. It is, moreover, a rough equivalent to other similar sayings of Jesus, such as 'Take heart' or 'Be of good cheer' (Mk. 6.50, Mt. 14.27). The words 'good pleasure' and 'flock' are not specifically Lucan, and much in the saying links it up with other sayings of Jesus—the use of 'Fear not', '*Father*' as the name for God, the thought of people in their relation to God as being like sheep. The precise phrase about God 'giving' the kingdom is not found elsewhere, but there are many other sayings which emphsaise *the initiative of God*, in bringing the kingdom to human life. And even if the word 'give' is not found often in sayings of Jesus about the kingdom, its correlative 'receive' does occur several times.

So this saying which speaks of God as 'giving' the kingdom belongs to that group of sayings about the kingdom which proclaim it as *coming* or 'being brought' into people's lives. It is one of the sayings of Jesus which lends support to Paul's emphatic doctrine of 'free grace'. There is also the recurring link of the thought of God as *Father* with the idea of the Kingdom.

20. Lk. 17.20–21:

The Kingdom of God is not coming with signs to be observed, nor will they say, 'Lo, here it is!' or 'There!', for behold the Kingdom of God is within you (or 'in the midst of you').

There is almost universal agreement that this particular saying is authentic. Its attitude to signs and omens is characteristic of Jesus, but sharply different from the attitude of his contemporaries, and also different from the thinking of the early Church, which was very interested in 'signs'. There is, however, a sharp dispute about its precise meaning, particularly about the translation of the Greek word *entos*. Some translate it as 'within', others as 'among'. It is an error, however, to rely on the fact that Luke describes the saying as spoken in reply to a question posed by a Pharisee as a determining factor in its interpretation. It is likely that the saying had an independent existence in the oral tradition and that Luke himself set it in this particular context. We learn from other episodes in the story of Jesus that his contemporaries were deeply interested in 'signs' that would give some hint about the hidden future. The Pharisees certainly shared this interest, but it would be by no means confined to them.

The general belief in Judaism at that time was that in due course God would assert himself against all evil and destroy it, and then establish his kingdom. It was also believed that this great day would also be preceded by certain recognisable signs of its approach—wars and rumours of war, etc. (cf. Mk. 13.7)—and people with special insight into the ways of God would be able to give warning of its nearness by reading the signs. Jesus was known to speak frequently about the Kingdom of God, and many hearers would tend to assume without further enquiry that to him as to them it meant only this coming Day of God. Someone might well have asked him how people could know when it was about to happen. His reply was quite at variance with anything they might have been expecting. He replied that there are no outward signs to warn people of the approach of God's Kingdom. Watching for visible hints would not be of any use at all. There would be nothing external one could point to as an omen of its arrival. Why? Because the Kingdom of God is not something which a man can see with his physical eyes, nor locate in some geographical area. The Kingdom of God is *entos* you.

The traditional translation of this Greek word *entos* is 'within' though modern commentators often prefer 'among'. Such a meaning would be in accord with the other teaching of Jesus. He spoke of his healing work among his fellows as evidence that the kingdom is 'among' them. But the appropriateness of 'among' should not of itself be sufficient ground for ruling out 'within', especially when on grammatical grounds it is the almost obvious meaning. Because 'within' is theologically unexpected is not an adequate ground for rejecting it. All the evidence points to the fact that Jesus was startlingly different from the conventional leaders of his day. It may well be that the facets of his character and teaching which are at variance with contemporary thought are those to which we should give greatest heed.

We may not be able to decide whether Jesus in the saying meant us to understand him to mean 'within' or 'among'. But whichever of the two is accepted, there can be no doubt that it is saying emphatically that the kingdom is actually present in the ministry of Jesus. It is not just something to be looked for in the future.

21. Lk. 18.29:

Truly I tell you that there is no one who has left house, wife, brothers, parents or children for the sake of the Kingdom of God who will not receive much more in this present time and in the age to come eternal life.

This is a saying which is based on Mk. 10.29,30, as also is Mt. 19.29. Luke, however, is the only one of the three who introduces the phrase 'Kingdom of God'. Mark expresses the motivation behind the great renunciation which the disciples have made as 'for my sake and the sake of the Gospel', and Matthew has 'for my name's sake'. Usually where Matthew or Luke makes changes in sayings recorded in Mark, we suspect that they are editing the material in a direction further away from what Jesus actually said in favour of their own preferences. It is possible, however, that occasionally an editorial change may bring a saying back nearer to its original form.

If this were (in part, at any rate) a genuine saying of Jesus, it would be completely in harmony with other sayings of his. The kingdom, we have already learnt, does require of those who seek a place in it, the *sacrifice* not only of evil things but also of good things, if they dispute God's rule in our lives. But also there has been the promise that the sacrifice once made leads to *gains* far greater than anything which has been sacrificed. The treasure in the field and the pearl of great price are abundantly worth what has to be paid for them. These same features are found in this saying also. One would very much like to know whether the allocation of the promised reward partly to 'this present time' and partly to 'the age to come' actually goes back to Jesus. It certainly was the way the New Testament as a whole came to understand his message.

It is interesting to note that in the mind of the evangelist the phrases 'for my sake', 'for the sake of the Gospel', 'for my name's sake', and 'for the sake of the Kingdom of God' all meant much the same thing.

Finally we must look at sayings of Jesus about the kingdom which occur in a fourth group—those which are recorded only in Matthew. We cannot help approaching this group with a certain degree of scepticism, as we try to determine how many of them have a good claim to authenticity. Of all the synoptic writers Matthew is clearly the one who exercises the greatest degree of freedom in editing the material he is reproducing, and in imposing his own interpretations upon it. We have already noted how he has devised a set formula

43

for introducing many parables which he believes teach truths about the kingdom: 'The Kingdom of heaven is like . . .', and how he repeats Mk. 9.1, but alters it in such a way as to distort its meaning quite seriously. In other respects also (not precisely concerned with the Kingdom of God) he allows his own strong feelings at certain points so to colour his material as seriously to misrepresent Jesus. For instance, in Mark, Matthew's main source, there is only one single instance where Jesus refers to some Pharisees as 'hypocrites', 'play-actors' (Mk. 7.6). In that particular context the word is appropriate. It refers to certain ritual actions (supposedly done to please God) which Pharisees carried out with exaggerated elaboration and consummate artistry. They were clearly doing it all, however, not to please and honour God, but to impress other people and show off their own knowledge of liturgical orthodoxy and accurate gestures. Matthew, however, transforms this one incident into a kind of running vendetta on the part of Jesus against the Pharisees. In Mark Jesus uses the word 'hypocrite' only once. Matthew, on the other hand, places it on the lips of Jesus no less than fourteen times. He makes chapter 23 into one long denunciation of 'hypocrites' (the word itself occurring there seven times). There is little doubt that this re-iteration of the stinging word 'hypocrite' is characteristic of Matthew and his own hostile attitude to Pharisees; but it is unlikely to be a true representation of Jesus. In this particular Matthew has done Jesus a serious disservice.

Similarly, in the sayings-material common to Matthew and Luke there is one incident where Jesus is represented as quoting the saying: 'There will be weeping and gnashing of teeth'. In Luke 13.28 the phrase fits naturally into the context. Jesus has been saying that foreigners will be welcomed into the Kingdom of God, and Jews will find themselves excluded (though they had assumed that they would have an automatically guaranteed place). They will feel overwhelmed with chagrin and incredulous dismay, they will 'weep and gnash their teeth'. It is a symbol of intense, unbearable disappointment—but not necessarily meant as a description of hell. In this same context Matthew (at 8.11) adds the idea that the rejected Jews will be in 'outer darkness', introducing a new eschatological note to the original saying. Moreover he re-introduces this threatening phrase about 'weeping and gnashing of teeth' to characterise the punishments of hell on no fewer than five other occasions (13.42, 13.50, 22.13, 24.51, 25.30). This multiplication of a threatening phrase and its use as a reference to hell has made the teaching of Jesus in parts sound very harsh and vindictive. Yet we can be pretty sure that this vindictiveness was in fact the characteristic of Matthew's teaching, not that of Jesus, and in thus distorting and exaggerating this feature he has done disservice to Jesus.

These recognisable tendencies in Matthew to embellish and exaggerate make us slow to accept as wholly authentic sayings of Jesus which are found only in Matthew. We shall need first to convince ourselves that a saying is free from any of Matthew's particular quirks and fancies. There are, however, two or three of these sayings about the kingdom which very probably do preserve authentic material.

22. Mt. 19.12

There are eunuchs who have been so from birth, and there are eunuchs who have been made eunuchs by men, and there are eunuchs who have made themselves eunuchs for the sake of the Kingdom of heaven.

With some misgiving we include this saying among those with a right to be regarded as authentic. There is every sign that Matthew received it as an independent saying, since it is only casually associated with the words which precede it. There is a general similarity in subject-matter but no integral link between them. There is, however, nothing to suggest that Matthew or his church invented this saying as a means of explaining what precedes it, or to support some favourite concern. The preceding words record Jesus's prohibition of divorce (except on grounds of the wife's sexual unfaithfulness). The only link between Mt. 19.12 and the preceding verse is that both are concerned with sexual matters. Matthew makes no suggestion about the actual situation in which Jesus spoke these words, so one has to try to guess what the circumstances may have been. It would appear that Jesus had been asked about celibacy and its place in the purposes of God for his servants. Jesus replies with this threefold answer: Some must accept celibacy because of a physical defect with which they were born; others have been castrated by people with power over them, for their own purposes; others voluntarily choose celibacy because they feel that thereby they can offer a more complete devotion to God's purposes without the distraction of any other loyalty. This voluntarily accepted deprivation is here expressed as being 'for the sake of the Kingdom of heaven'.

There are certain features of the saying which make it sound authentic to Jesus. In external form there is the threefoldness which appears so frequently in the recorded words of Jesus. In its internal content it coincides with other words of Jesus which appear to be authentic, for instance Mk. 9.43–47 about the sacrifice of foot, hand or eye in order to gain entrance to the kingdom. It meant that 'for the sake of the Kingdom of God'—in order that a man may do God's will with complete single-mindedness—there are some who will feel constrained to renounce all sexual relationships, even the normal and natural fulfilment in marriage, home and family. Another saying of Jesus which carries a similar emphasis to this is that found in Lk. 18.29 (discussed in section 21) where Jesus speaks of a disciple leaving home and wife and other relations 'for the sake of the Kingdom of God'.

This consistency of form and content with the general teaching of Jesus makes it likely that this saying is a genuine one.

23. Mt. 21.31:

Truly I say to you that tax collectors and harlots go into the Kingdom of God before you.

One feature which immediately suggests that this saying has not been subjected to Matthaean revision is that it speaks of the Kingdom of *God*. Matthew himself much prefers the phrase 'Kingdom of *heaven*'. Clearly therefore this saying must have come to Matthew in this form and for some reason he omitted to bring it into line with his normal usage. The saying also opens with a phrase very characteristic of Jesus: 'Truly (Amen) I say to you'. Again, one of the undisputed, historical truths about Jesus is that he showed himself the friend and champion of the social outcasts of his time, and was denounced for it by the leaders of the established religion as 'friend of taxgatherers and sinners'. So this word about them is entirely compatible with all we know of Jesus from other sources. It not only expresses his feeling of friendship for them, but also says that some of them will gain entrance to the kingdom in preference to Jewish leaders, who took it for granted as their right. It expresses the same point of view as Mt. 8.11 = Lk. 13.29 (section 14).

There is also the common phrase about '*entering*' the kingdom, and implied teaching about the qualities which facilitate entrance—a sense of unworthiness and poverty of spirit—and the qualities which prove to be barriers—pride, self-sufficiency and self-righteousness.

24. Mt. 23.13:

Woe to you scribes and Pharisees, hypocrites, because you shut the Kingdom of heaven against men; for you do not enter yourselves, nor allow those who would enter to go in.

This saying comes from what has been called that 'hateful chapter' in which Matthew has gathered together the words of Jesus about the Pharisees, and given to them a note of contempt and denunciation which they did not at first contain, by thrusting into them again and again the stinging word 'hypocrite'. We believe there are good grounds for rejecting the authenticity of the word 'hypocrite' in this particular saying. It is, however, certain that Jesus did speak critical words of the Pharisees (even if he did not frequently use the word 'hypocrite') because at their worst they represented that attitude towards God which Jesus deplored and wished to change. So far as human action was concerned they thought of God's will as concerned with obedience to rules about diet, ritual cleanliness, sabbath-keeping, etc. For Jesus it was something quite different. It was a compassionate concern for the welfare of men and women. His thought of the Kingdom of God had little to do with religious rules and rituals. The healing of mentally-afflicted people was for him a clear sign that God's rule had asserted itself in their lives. For the Pharisees because of his indifference towards their ritual demands it was a sign of his co-operation with Satan. It may well have been these two characteristics of the Pharisees, their legalism that made them callous to human need and their prejudice which made them mistake God's healing work for Satan's manoeuvres, that led Jesus to rebuke them not only for not entering the kingdom themselves but also, by their example and teaching, for making it hard for others to enter. Elsewhere Jesus has spoken of wrong attitudes in man which can prevent him from entering the kingdom. This saying is a salutary reminder that our attitude may not only exclude ourselves, but lead to the exclusion of others. Elsewhere Jesus spoke stern words about millstones to those who put hindrances in the way of 'little ones'.

25. Mt. 25.34:

Come, O blessed of my Father, inherit the Kingdom prepared for you from the foundation of the world.

The parable of the sheep and goats is something of an enigma. The spirit and content of the parable as a whole is strikingly true to the essential teaching of Jesus; yet its framework contains many signs of Matthew's editorial work. For instance, there is the phrase about 'the Son of Man coming in glory along with the angels', (25.31), which is very Matthaean. There is also the figure of the king. Nowhere, except in Matthew, does a king appear in any of the parables of Jesus, whereas Matthew brings a king into three of them. The emphasis on 'eternal punishment' (25.46) and 'eternal fire' prepared for the 'cursed' (25.41) is again characteristic of Matthew. It is, however, difficult to believe that verses 35–40 (apart from the figure of the king) do not come from Jesus, as also verses 42–45. It is an essential and recurring element in the teaching of Jesus that love for God and love for one's neighbour are so closely intertwined as to be almost identical, and that one's neighbour is anyone at all whose need comes to our notice (such as that of an injured stranger, even a foreigner, at the roadside, Lk. 10.36). Matthew makes the story into a representation of the Last Judgement. It is, however, clear that the purpose of the parable is not really to teach anything very precise about the Last Judgement. Rather it is using the symbol of the Last Judgement to emphasise in the strongest possible way those actions here on earth which God most warmly commends and those which he condemns. It is all about the kind of conduct God asks of his followers NOW.

At 25.34 the verdict on 'the righteous' is: 'Come, O blessed of my Father, inherit the Kingdom prepared for you from the foundation of the world'. How far can this be regarded as a genuine saying of Jesus? The phrase: 'prepared for you from the foundation of the world' sounds rather more technical and 'theological' than the language Jesus uses elsewhere. But the parable seems to require some word of address to 'the righteous'. The words *come* and *blessed* are entirely appropriate to Jesus; so too the reference to God as *Father.* What of the phrase 'inherit the Kingdom'? The association of Father and Kingdom has already been met frequently in the teaching of Jesus, and though the word 'inherit' does not occur elsewhere in his teaching with the kingdom, it is found with 'eternal life', which closely corresponds with the kingdom. Oddly enough the phrase 'inherit the Kingdom' occurs four times in Paul's writings. Did Paul use it because he found it in the tradition which came from Jesus, or did Matthew and Paul use it because they were familiar with it as a phrase in use in the post-resurrection Church? There is no clear answer. The kingdom here has a future reference, but it sounds more like a 'place' to which men go beyond death than an apocalyptic event in which the kingdom bursts in upon the world of men.

We cannot be sure about the authenticity of this saying about the kingdom. But if the central part of the parable is genuine and if its association with the Kingdom of God is also authentic, then we may find here hints about what Jesus regarded as qualifications for a place in God's Kingdom. Already childlikeness and poverty (of spirit) have been mentioned. Here the essential quality commended is that of practical compassion offered to bring relief to human need and distress even to complete strangers, and it is offered not with any thought of reward or in a spirit of self-congratulation, but humbly without any awareness that anything out of the ordinary is being done. This quality characterises the 'righteous' who find themselves offered the kingdom as their rightful inheritance.

The Parables

It is generally agreed that the parables of Jesus preserve much that is authentically the teaching of Jesus. Their background accurately reflects the conditions of Palestine at that time, and in themselves they are in the main strikingly fresh and natural, when compared with the somewhat laboured parabolic teaching of the rabbis. Moreover their content is entirely consistent with what we know from other sources of the teaching and ministry of Jesus.

Some of these parables were undoubtedly spoken to bring out and emphasise some truth about the Kingdom of God. The parable of the mustard seed, for instance, (in Mk. 4.30 and parallels) and the parable of the leaven (Lk. 13.20) are both explicitly related to the kingdom, in order to illustrate and emphasise the irrepressible inner vitality of the Kingdom. In each case the parable is introduced by a question, which we have already noted is a recurring characteristic in the teaching of Jesus: 'To what shall we compare the Kingdom of God?'. These are the only two parables which are explicitly related to the kingdom, apart from several in Matthew which begin with the formula: 'The Kingdom of Heaven is like ...'. Sometimes, however, this formula is unsuitable for what follows in the parable, and is not found in the same parable in the other gospels. It is most unlikely to go back to Jesus himself, and must be regarded as a formula which Matthew himself attached to certain parables where he felt it fitted. It is quite possible that some of these parables were indeed spoken by Jesus to enforce some aspect of the kingdom, and that Matthew was right in trying to indicate this. But it would be quite wrong to apply all these parables from Matthew to the kingdom merely because Matthew chose to introduce them with his standard formula.

A number of the parables, however, can be most naturally understood in the context of the ministry of Jesus as being used to emphasise and make real some truth about the Kingdom of God. As we have seen, the parables of the mustard seed and the leaven portray the inner vitality of the kingdom. The parables of the hidden treasure and the pearl of great price illuminate for us the appropriate response in man to the realisation that the kingdom is there for the taking. This response consists of an almost reckless abandon in his readiness to let everything else go if only the supreme privilege of the kingdom may become his. It is just one further instance of the insistence of Jesus, which we have already noted, on the need for a man to be totally committed to God's way, whatever the cost, if the full life of the kingdom is to be his.

The two parables of the tower builder and the king setting out to battle stress that this commitment to God's way must not be a blind, unconsidered, emotional response to an idealistic call, but a commitment made with eyes wide open to the cost involved. Total commitment is required but it must be a total commitment which is realistically accepted. The newness of the kingdom as compared with the old Jewish legalistic system is brought out in the parables of the patch and the wineskins.

There are several parables whose main thrust is the need for constant alertness lest God's moment present itself in our lives and find us unprepared, so that the opportunity passes by and is lost. Such parables are the watchman (Mk. 13.33-37), the burglar (Mt. 24.43f.), the servant in authority (Mt. 24.45-51), and the ten virgins (Mt. 25.1-13). In the gospels these are often made to refer to the future Parousia and the need to be alert and ready when that great moment comes; but in the actual ministry of Jesus it is much more likely that they referred to the coming of God's Kingdom in the proclamation and ministry of Jesus. Jesus proclaimed: '*Now* is the accepted time', and urged on his hearers the need to seize God's offered moment without delay. If God's approach is ignored through unreadiness or indecision, it may be lost for ever. It cannot be re-arranged at a later time just to suit man's convenience. The opportunity may be quite

51

unrepeatable, and so there is the most pressing urgency in that particular moment, a crisis captured in other famous words:

> There is a tide in the affairs of men,
> Which taken at the flood leads on to fortune;
> Omitted, all the voyage of their life,
> Is bound in shallows and in miseries.

So close is the link between many of the parables and the message of the kingdom that Perrin (in *Jesus and the Language of the Kingdom*, p. 39) goes so far as to say that 'all the parables have as their ultimate referent the Kingdom of God'. Unless, however, we assume that everything that Jesus ever said or did can legitimately be linked with the Kingdom of God, this is clearly an exaggeration. Some of the parables arise out of aspects of the ministry of Jesus not directly linked with the kingdom.

There have been many very able expositions of what the Kingdom of God means in the gospels. Most of these, however, have tended to base their conclusions on all the sayings in the gospels about the kingdom (often combining them with sayings about the Son of Man). In their totality, however, these include not only authentic sayings of Jesus, but also others which bear clear marks of editorial activity, and which in their present form reflect the mind of of the redactor rather than that of Jesus himself. Here we have tried in the first place to separate off the sayings of Jesus which may be regarded as authentic and to make these the basis of our primary study. It was what Jesus meant by the kingdom which is what we most want to find out. The editorial emphases, often referred to as 'redaction', have, however, their own importance, and will be considered at a later stage.

3. THE FEATURES OF THE KINGDOM OF GOD

The very essence of the Kingdom of God, the basic assumption behind every thought about it, is that wherever the kingdom is there God rules and commands, and his subjects accept his authority and give him total obedience. This is so basic in the teaching of Jesus, indeed implicit in the very phrase 'Kingdom of God', that it is assumed as a truth too obvious to need spelling out in detail.

We note again that the phrase 'Kingdom of God' is just a manner of speaking. It really means 'God as he exercises his rightful authority to rule'. When we read: 'The Kingdom of God has burst in upon you', it is not in fact a Kingdom which is on the move, but God himself, as rightful ruler of the world, who is confronting human life, challenging it, seeking to restore it, taking it under his control. 'To enter the Kingdom', therefore, means to allow one's life to be brought under the ruling power of God. When Jesus speaks of the kingdom as 'coming' it is a means of directing man's attention to a new and vigorous initiative which God is taking, an initiative in which Jesus believes himself to be totally involved, and of which he sees his ministry as an integral part. It is action by God which is making possible a new relationship between God and man.

We need to remind ourselves of the background against which Jesus proclaimed this message. The general belief in Judaism at that time was that God, though unquestionably the rightful ruler of his people, was no longer in effective control of his world. His rightful power and authority had been usurped by evil powers. This, however, could be regarded only as a temporary setback, not a final defeat. In due course, at the time which God saw to be the right time, God would re-assert his authority and come into the world to claim what rightly belonged to him. This, when it happened, would be a time of great rejoicing for his faithful people, and a time of dismay and humiliation for his enemies, whether human or superhuman. But at the moment evil was rampant and the time of God's coming intervention seemed remote and far distant in the future. Meanwhile the official teaching of the religious leaders was that God's faithful people must wait for God's moment in patient hope, humbly offering to God obedience to the laws which he had given, believing that the greater their obedience the sooner would be his coming in deliverance. That coming deliverance was visualised in different ways. Sometimes it was seen as a great spiritual renewal of the nation of Israel within the course of history; at other times it was spoken of as something that would coincide with the end of this present world order and the establishment of something quite different—a new earth and a new heaven. Not all people accepted the official line of 'patient hope'. There were some activists who believed that violent action against those whom they saw as the agents of the powers of evil could bring nearer and hasten that hoped-for day. There were others who believed that this great day was quite near and that special signs would soon indicate its approach; some claimed that secret knowledge of what these signs would be had been given to them and were eagerly alert to discern those signs. But for the most part people thought that the day of hope was far away in some distant future; the best they could do was to practise patience and humble obedience.

Since God appeared to be no longer effective master in his own world, it could only be that somehow his enemies had got the better of him, if only temporarily. These enemies were evil spirits or demons, with Satan as their supreme ruler. At the time of Jesus there was a widespread assumption that Satan had managed to establish control in the earth, and from that vantage point was able to dominate the life of men. When therefore God comes in power to claim again the world which belongs to him, it can only be done by the overthrow and disablement of Satan (cf. Lk. 11.22). So Jesus, in a moment of striking success in his own mission and that of his disciples, describes the achievement in terms of the destruction of Satan: 'I saw Satan fallen as lightning from heaven' (Lk. 10.18).

1. The essence of the message of Jesus was that God's chosen time had arrived—NOW. His kingdom was already breaking into the world of men. This was no longer a promise for some distant future for which men must wait with a hope so slender that it soon dwindles into apathy. God's action had begun. Men must awaken to the truth of it, and respond eagerly and actively. Satan's realm was already threatened, invaded and about to be conquered. The distant hope was already being swallowed up in present reality. NOW was the moment of God's action, and the time for man to act in response. Men were summoned to identify themselves with this coming of God's Kingdom, and to make themselves God's instruments in its coming. Their response is demanded urgently, without delay, without hesitation, without misgiving.

The fact that *God is actively breaking into the life of the world* is expressed in such terms as these: The Kingdom 'has drawn near', 'is coming', 'will come', 'has burst upon', 'is forcing itself into' (as in §§ **1**, **3**, **11**, **15**, **16**). Sometimes this coming refers to what is soon to happen, sometimes to what has already taken place. How far, in this context, God's action is to be regarded as past, present or future will be discussed later. The main point, however, is that Jesus proclaimed that God is now taking the initiative, not at some distant time in the future, but NOW. Part of the immediate evidence of this advance of the kingdom is seen in the power of Jesus to drive out demons which have been maiming human lives (Mt. 12.28). A seriously disabled woman, described as one who had been long 'bound by Satan' (Lk. 13.16), is healed, and the power of Satan to cripple her is broken. These victories of God over Satan are likened to the success of an invading force: a strong man, long in occupation of another's property, is having to vacate it, because the rightful owner has come to reclaim it with strength that cannot be withstood.

Further emphasis on God's initiative in the coming of the

kingdom is found in the instances where the kingdom is spoken of as something which God 'gives' to man. This kingdom is not to be thought of as something which man by his skill or determination can manipulate and organise. It is something which God *gives* (see §§ **9** and **10**) and man receives.

2. This same truth about God's present, effective activity in his world is also expressed in terms of *the bursting vitality of this Kingdom* (see §§ **2**, **15**, **16**, **17**). This is brought out in the figurative language which represents the kingdom as something of an inner, expanding (almost explosive) energy. This kingdom is not to be thought of as an established, static entity, but as a centre of radiating power. It is like a mustard seed, reputed to be the smallest of all seeds, and yet possessed of such extraordinary inner powers that from it will come in the course of a few short weeks a plant big enough to be mistaken for a tree. It is like leaven, which when compared with the huge baking of flour into which it is mixed is only a small fragment, but within an hour or so it can transform the quality of the whole mass by the vitality of its active presence. Similarly in Mk. 4.26 the seed whose mysterious inner powers enable it to grow secretly and unaided by man is seen as a symbol of God's power in the world. Man can only look and wonder and gratefully accept the benefits it brings. It is misleading to speak of these parables as 'parables of growth'. Growth suggests something gradual and slow. But this is not the emphasis here. Rather it is that something which in the beginning appears small and unpromising does in fact produce results out of all proportion to its original size, and produces them with astonishing speed. So the kingdom may seem insignificant in its beginnings, and largely unnoticed in its operation, but can nevertheless prove vigorously effective in its results.

3. For those who accept the kingdom it is found to be *a concentration of blessing*, though blessings very different in quality from those acclaimed by worldly standards (§§ **10**, **12**, **13**, **14**, **16**, **21**, **24**). Indeed participation in the kingdom often

involves the loss of what, by conventional standards, would be regarded as life's most attractive rewards and pleasures. But whatever may be their deprivations, even the 'poor' are pronounced 'blessed' because they have received the kingdom, and that more than compensates for all other losses (Mt. 5.3). Their privileges exceed those of John the Baptist even though by God's standards he was the greatest of all men who had lived up to that time (Mt. 11.11). They include the favour of enjoying the company of the greatest men of Israel's past (Mt. 8.11,12). For those who receive the kingdom, it brings health and true happiness, both here in this life and in the life beyond this one (Mt. 6.33, 12,28, Lk. 18.29). It consists of happy relationships within God's family, with God as Father and with all his people as brothers and sisters.

4. Some references to the kingdom imply that it has *a future dimension* (§§ **3, 7**). Whatever may be the extent of the present operation of the kingdom, it is only a first instalment. Much more is to come. So the disciples are urged to pray for its coming. Compared with what has already happened during the ministry of Jesus, that coming will be 'with power' (Mk. 9.1). The disciples of Jesus will in the future be enabled to do even greater things than he has done. Some, however, think that this 'coming with power' indicates something of an entirely different dimension, a supernatural intervention. This future coming of the kingdom, whatever form it may take, will, however, reach out far beyond its restricted beginning in Israel. People from other, foreign, nations will be brought in (Mt. 8.11), and that splendid future will be such as to merit description as a celebration banquet (Mt. 8.11). Similarly as Jesus drinks wine at the Last Supper he speaks of it as his last taste of wine on earth. His next taste will be when he 'drinks it new' in the Kingdom of God (Mk. 14.25). Joy, happiness and celebration mark the future of the kingdom.

5. In view of the insistence by some scholars that for Jesus the kingdom was entirely an event of the future, it is sur-prising to find so few of these authentic sayings which un-mistakably refer to the future. It is true that in some areas of

the teaching ascribed to Jesus in the synoptics there is clear reference to some future dénouement, especially to the coming of the Son of Man in glory. But this type of saying does not occur in relation to these genuine sayings about the kingdom. In by far the greater number of the sayings under consideration, the reference to the kingdom is more easily understood as a present reference, as though the Kingdom is in some sense already present, at least incipiently, in the ministry of Jesus. Some indeed, beyond any doubt, do treat the kingdom as a present fact (§§ **1**, **6**, **8**, **10**, **14**, **15**, **20**, **25**).

The most indisputable of the *present references to the Kingdom* is the excerpt considered in section 16 (Mt. 12.28 = Lk. 11.20). There Jesus explicitly declares that his own power to heal lives afflicted with demon-possession is an indication that God's Kingdom has burst in upon them.

Similarly in section 16, though the verb used is one whose meaning is uncertain (Greek *biazetai*), what is beyond doubt is that the tense of the verb is in the present. It is used to describe something actually taking place in the present time. Moreover, in Lk. 47.21 (section 20) however the ambiguous Greek word *entos* is understood, the verb again is in the present tense. The Kingdom *is* here, whether it be 'among' or 'within' you. Further the words about the kingdom in other sayings clearly apply to an actually present situation (see §§ **6**, **8**, **10**, **14**, **22**).

There is also the disputed meaning of 'has drawn near' in § **1**. In the light, however, of the unmistakable presence of the kingdom in so many other words of Jesus, the declaration by Jesus at the beginning of his ministry (and at the time the disciples went out on mission) that 'the Kingdom of God has drawn near' must mean that the kingdom was so near as to be actively at work almost immediately, if not actually present at the time of speaking. Even if it did mean only 'near' when the ministry began, it meant near enough to be actually present as the work of the ministry unfolded.

We shall need to look again at this issue of the future aspect of the kingdom, since it has so often been claimed to be the dominating feature of all the teaching of Jesus. At the moment we note that two of the four future references to the kingdom

(§§ **3**, **5**, **7**, **13**) could simply refer to a life with God beyond death, and the other two to the extension and intensification of God's rule upon the earth which followed the ministry of Jesus. There is nothing compellingly apocalyptic about any of them.

6. The most prominent emphasis in the sayings of Jesus about the kingdom is that God is taking action. The message of the kingdom is about what God is doing—asserting his authority, laying claim to what rightly belongs to him, overthrowing forces of evil which resist him. Yet in spite of this there is no suggestion that man in the face of God's actions becomes just a leaf driven by the wind, with no will or choice of his own. Man, it is true, is being made to feel the awesome pressure of God upon his life, the overpowering claims of God's demands, as though God is taking charge and there is little man can do about it. But in fact the whole encounter *awaits man's response* (§§ **4**, **5**, **6**, **8**, **18**, **21**, **22**, **23**, **24**, **25**). He can in the last resort turn his back upon God's approach, and shut up his life against it. The words which describe man's act of saying 'Yes' or 'No' to God are, however, usually words which indicate a response to something God has first done rather than words which suggest man's spontaneous initiative. Man may 'enter' the kingdom (§§ **4**, **5**, **6**, **22**, **23**). But it is already there, near at hand, just one step away, though the final decisive step must indeed be his. Man may 'receive' the kingdom (§§ **4**, **21**). It is there as a gift or an opportunity for him to take, but it is not forced on him. One word suggesting human initiative is in fact used: man is bidden to 'seek' (or 'seek first') the kingdom (§ **12**). In its original meaning, however, probably even this does not suggest that the kingdom is something which can only be found after much searching. Rather it is the command that the disciple who has already received the kingdom should put its interests first in every decision he is called upon to make. The kingdom must count for more than even the basic needs of physical life. The same emphasis is found in the word of Jesus warning that one who is always 'looking back' is not fit for the Kingdom of God.

There are other sayings of Jesus about the kingdom which make it clear that the kingdom is not 'irresistible grace', but that man has his part to play. These are the sayings which emphasise the costly sacrifice that may be required if a man is to enter the kingdom (§§ 5, 6, 18, 21, 25). If he cannot face the sacrifice, there is no place for him in the kingdom. Hand, foot, eye, wealth, home, parents, family all have to be subordinated to the kingdom, if the kingdom is to have its rightful place in a man's life.

7. There is some information in these sayings of Jesus about the *qualities in human life* which enable a man to make the right, the positive response to God's call. The one which is most emphasised is an eager readiness to venture out—not with a cautious, conditional, provisional acceptance, but with wholehearted and final commitment, indeed a total abandonment of self to God, as with a man who sells all that he has to gain a supreme treasure. It must, however, be an open-eyed commitment which recognises and counts the cost without any illusions, and so is not daunted by unexpected difficulties. It is a readiness to subordinate everything to the rule of the kingdom, even things in themselves good, but capable of diverting a man from his supreme loyalty (§§ 5, 6, 18, 21, 25).

This too is an emphasis found elsewhere in the teaching of Jesus, who calls on men to be ready to say 'No' to self (deny self), to choose the narrow gate and the restricted path, to 'leave the dead to bury their own dead', to sell everything and follow Jesus.

Other qualities commended as conducive to the life of the kingdom are 'childlikeness' and 'poverty' (of spirit?) (§§ 4, 6, 13). It would help us if we could define with greater precision just what these qualities meant for Jesus. Perhaps one way of sensing their meaning is to learn from the lives of outstanding disciples of Christ who seem most to reflect the standards of Christ himself—people like St Francis of Assisi in the Middle Ages or Mother Teresa in our own. In their presence we ask: Do 'childlikeness' and 'poverty' imply a happy freedom from the tyranny of conventional values and standards and social proprieties, a complete disregard for the worship of wealth and high wages and material prosperity which so dominate mankind? Does it include what elsewhere in the New Testament is called freedom from 'respect for persons', from the custom of treating people differently according to their class and social standing?

8. Just as an eager readiness for total commitment, along with 'childlikeness' and 'poverty', opens the way for entry into the kingdom, so an absence of these qualities or faults consisting of their opposites may bar the way (§§ **6, 22**). An inclination towards compromise, when the issue is one between God and his enemies, is such a fault. So too is spiritual pride and an undue sense of one's own religious superiority, so that harlots and taxgatherers find their way into the kingdom more readily than Pharisees. Awareness of one's own spiritual achievements and a desire to have them noted by others, whether God or man, is also a serious obstacle. Better far is that attitude of mind which, 'when you have carried out all your orders' says: 'We are servants and deserve no credit; we have only done our duty'.

9. There are other features of the kingdom which should be noted. One is its *newness* (§ **14**). Though Jesus assessed John the Baptist to be even greater than any of the great men of the past, yet he belonged to *that* past, and the Kingdom of God belonged to a new future, and there were privileges denied to John which were the prerogative of even the humblest participant within the kingdom. It was something for which the past had no equivalent. This tallies with other sayings of Jesus which emphasise the newness of what he had come to inaugurate. He had come not merely to patch up and repair the old ideas of man's relationship to God, but to renew them fundamentally. Some of his parabolic sayings illustrate this.

Besides being something which is strikingly new compared with the old and outworn religious system which it replaces, the kingdom is *universal* in its range and availability (§ **13**). No one is excluded by reason of race or social class. Spiritual qualities alone are the qualifications for entry. People will come from the east and from the west, people from all nations, to claim their place in it, whereas those who regard themselves as leaders of God's own people will find themselves excluded. Not only foreigners find their way into the kingdom before the recognised leaders of the Jewish nation's life, but so do social outcasts, taxgatherers and sinners. So elsewhere in the teaching and life of Jesus we find this same openness to men and women of all races and social classes although the religious officials of that time found it most offensive and declared it to be religiously most irregular. They sneered at him as 'the friend of publicans and sinners'; he incurred their anger by making hated Samaritans examples of commendable conduct (Lk. 10.33ff., 17.16), and even dared to befriend and visit a member of the hated Roman army of occupation (Mt. 8.5ff.) and commended his faith.

We noted earlier that the Kingdom is identified with 'blessings' of various kinds. It is also found frequently in close association with other words used to describe special spiritual privilege. One such word is 'life' (see §§ 5 and 21). In (§ 5) life is introduced as a natural synonym for the kingdom and in (§ 21) it is the privilege of those who are in the kingdom. This again is in line with the rest of the teaching of Jesus where life is regarded as the great privilege which God wishes to make available to men (Mk. 9.43, 10.17; Mt. 7.14, 18.8; Lk. 10.20, 18.18).

If life is used as a kind of synonym for the kingdom, then the thought of God as Father is a correlative of it. In this group of twenty-five sayings four are specifically associated with the word *Father* (§§ 11, 12, 19, 24). There can be no doubt that this way of speaking of God was markedly characteristic of Jesus; he even used that peculiarly intimate word for 'Father'—*Abba*. It is, however, surprising to find this family word so firmly associated with sayings about the kingdom. Father and Kingdom belong to different areas of life, one to the home, the other to the nation. But it is to God as Father that Jesus bids men pray: 'Your Kingdom come'. It is also our Father who, we are assured, knows our human needs and will provide all life's necessities, provided we boldly put first in our lives the requirements of his kingdom. It is God as Father who will 'give' the kingdom to those who on their own would have no competence to claim it. Those whose quality of life proves that the power of the kingdom is already active in them are called 'you blessed of my Father'. The life of the kingdom, though marked by obedience in its subjects to the one who has the right to command, is also marked, in the lives both of the one who has the right to command and of the many who obey, by a relationship of affection and trust as that found between parent and child in a truly happy family.

These recurring parallels to the same features in other areas of the teaching of Jesus help to confirm the authenticity of these words about the kingdom.

Apocalyptic and the Kingdom of God

Among the twenty-five sayings of Jesus about the kingdom which we have treated as authentic, only four make unmistakable reference to the future, and none of them is specifically apocalyptic in its form or phraseology. This is surprising because it has often and emphatically been claimed that in the teaching of Jesus the kingdom was wholly an expectation for the future and also part of an apocalyptic view of the future. The dawn of the kingdom and the 'Second Coming' of Christ are regarded as part of the same cosmic event. There is, however, in these twenty-five sayings nothing to support this claim. The texts which are quoted in order to establish this association of the kingdom with the Parousia and to invest it with apocalyptic features are not the sayings which have the strongest claim to authenticity. Rather they are found in what appear as redactional passages mainly in Matthew, and to a lesser degree in Luke. They are usually sayings which are clearly adaptations of earlier forms of the tradition. They represent Matthew's (or Luke's) theological outlook rather than the mind of Jesus. We shall need to look further at this point when we examine Matthew's work as an editor, so far as it affects what he includes about the kingdom. Here we pause merely to remind ourselves of some facts already noted. Though Mt. 16.28 is clearly Matthew's reproduction of Mk. 9.1 it has been made strikingly different. Mark quotes

Jesus as saying that some of the bystanders will live to 'see the Kingdom of God having come with power'. Matthew changes this: what the bystanders will live to see is 'the Son of Man coming in his Kingdom'. The coming of the Son of Man is identified with the coming of the kingdom. Matthew may well have felt quite sure that he was merely saying more explicitly what was already implicit in Mark, but in fact he forced an apocalyptic interpretation on Mark's reported saying which was not originally part of it. Other passages in Matthew which appear to link the kingdom with the future coming of the Son of Man are, for example, 13.41, 25.31 and 34, 13.47–50. None of these seem to us to have any claim to authenticity, since they all reflect the features of Matthew's redactional activity (including his liking for 'weeping and gnashing of teeth').

Much less frequently than Matthew, Luke also, though on one occasion only, combines the Kingdom of God with the Coming of the Son of Man. But he acts in the reverse way to Matthew. Matthew introduces the Son of Man into a kingdom saying. Luke introduces the kingdom into a Son of Man saying. At Lk. 21.31 he repeats a saying about the Son of Man which he has found in Mk. 13.29 but introduces into it a reference also to the Kingdom of God. This association of Kingdom and Son of Man is due to Luke's editorial work.

There are, of course, apocalyptic sayings in Mark (e.g., Mk. 13.26,27, 14.62) as well as in Matthew, but these are not associated with the kingdom. Nor for that matter can they confidently be regarded as authentic sayings of Jesus. Some competent scholars view them as sayings which came into existence in the post-resurrection Church and were then read back on to the lips of Jesus. Certainly an apocalyptic mood of expectation gripped parts of the early Church. Paul's letters make this clear—especially his two letters to the Thessalonians. Scholars differ in their assessment of the relationship between the early Church and Jesus on this issue. Some argue that the early Church developed a belief in the Second Coming of Christ and then attributed it to Jesus himself and reported his sayings accordingly. Others contend that the presence of widespread apocalyptic expectations in the early

Church can only be explained by the belief that they did in fact receive it from Jesus. This, however, is less than wholly convincing because at that time other religious communities were imbued with apocalyptic hopes, and they did not receive them from Jesus. Apocalyptic concepts were in the air.

It has sometimes been argued that since apocalyptic expectations were abroad at the time of Jesus (as such writings as the Book of Enoch and those from Qumran show) therefore Jesus must have used the phrase 'the Kingdom of God' 'in the generally accepted sense' (so Perrin). This claim, however, that Jesus must have conformed to the 'generally accepted' ideas of some existing group of the time is highly questionable. It was by no means characteristic of Jesus to take over unaltered what he met in other contemporary groups. He found himself sharply at variance with the Pharisees on ways of observing the Mosaic Law, and he differed from the Sadducees on their belief about the after-life and on the administration of the Temple. He did not adopt the monastic isolation of the Qumran community, nor the militant patriotism of the zealots. He maintained also a firm independence even from John the Baptist, though he reverenced him more highly than any other man. It is, therefore, most unlikely that Jesus reproduced what the apocalyptists were saying about the kingdom, merely because they represented the popular craze of the moment.

If, of course, Jesus was an apocalyptic who spoke as he is recorded as doing in Mt. 16.28, than he was self-deceived, because the events he forecast did not take place as he said they would. Many scholars think that it is most unlikely that Jesus would be mistaken on a matter of such importance. There are also sayings attributed to Jesus of a very different type—anti-apocalyptic, in fact—in which he denies that any human being knows what lies in the future, and that it is wrong for his disciples to busy their heads trying to anticipate it (e.g., Mk. 13.32, Acts 1.7). Moreover some of his own sayings are the very opposite of apocalyptic—as when he says that God is a Father who sends his rain on the unjust and the just, including all people without distinction within his generous care; and that God is one who cares deeply for

65

each tiny sparrow and transient wild flower. Apocalyptic seems inconsistent with such emphases in his teaching. It is impossible to find an agreed solution, but if a provisional point of view must be adopted, we should regard Jesus as standing in the prophetic line of those who look for God's action within history on moral grounds rather than catastrophic events which bring history to an early end.

Interesting support has recently appeared for this non-apocalyptic view of Jesus in a book by a non-Christian writer, who presumably stands outside the controversies of Christian theologians. Dr Vermes in his book *Jesus the Jew* discusses the use by Jesus of the phrase 'Son of Man'. His conclusion is that the apocalyptic uses of this title in the gospels, that is those associating the Son of Man with the Parousia, are not authentic to Jesus; only those are authentic which refer to the Son of Man as a figure already active on earth. He bases his judgement on the use of the phrase in Galilean Aramaic.

Of the four sayings of Jesus about the kingdom (among our twenty-five) which have a future reference, two can best be understood as referring to what we commonly mean by 'heaven'—life with God beyond this earthly sphere—such as is found in other parts of the gospels. This is the sphere where God is permanently supreme, where his kingdom already exists, from whence it will in due course come to this earth.

The other two sayings—the prayer for God's Kingdom to come and the promises that some now alive will live to see the kingdom having come with power—though referring to the future do not sound at all apocalyptic. They fit into that mode of thought which visualises the Kingdom of God in the ministry of Jesus as 'a present reality working towards a future consummation' (T. W. Manson). The thought of Jesus is less that of the apocalyptists than of the ancient Jewish prayer: 'May God establish his kingdom during your life and during the life of all the house of Israel, even speedily and at a near time'. The proclamation of Jesus is that God has taken the first steps towards a full answer to that prayer. Men must continue to pray for the final success of what God has begun, for the splendid fulfilment of what is already

taking shape. Some indeed will live to see this kingdom powerfully present in their midst.

The idea that the coming of God's Kingdom is to be
identified with the future coming of the Son of Man on the
clouds and the end of the present world order is irreconcil-
able with all the sayings which clearly speak of the kingdom
as a powerful energy already present in the ministry of
Jesus (§§ **1, 6, 8, 10, 14, 15, 16, 20, 25**). Moreover such an
understanding of the kingdom as likens its activity to that of
the mustard seed (§ **2**) or leaven (§ **18**), does not fit an apocalyptic point of view. Nor do those sayings which indicate
qualities of character which help or hinder entrance into the
kingdom (§§ **4, 5, 6, 8**).

The basic teaching of Jesus about the kingdom does not
therefore support an apocalyptic interpretation of it. There is
another commonly affirmed emphasis about the kingdom
which is misleading and ought to be corrected. It is expressed in the claim that the kingdom is not 'psychological'.
Bundy affirmed that the kingdom is 'a cosmic event, *not
psychological*'. T. W. Manson, though using a different emphasis from Bundy on other matters, writes that the kingdom
is 'a fact of history, *not of psychology*', adding: 'The Kingdom
of heaven is a state of affairs not a state of mind'. We may
agree with the main concern of these writers that the Kingdom of God is not to be thought of as a kind of private
salvation known only to the individual through some inner
emotional experience, a heart-warming secret ecstasy which
has no reality apart from the inner life of the individual
involved. The Kingdom of God is *not* just this. It is above all
God's act in asserting his authority and right to rule, not
only in an individual's inner life, but in the whole area of life
within which that person lives. It is a fact of 'history' in
that the coming of God's Kingdom makes its mark on the
life of society and human relationships. But it is wrong to
add that this has no psychological content. God's action,
according to Jesus, becomes effective through human response.
It is not like an earthquake or a volcanic eruption or an
atom bomb which is a non-human upheaval on a massive
scale which takes no notice of human attitudes. It does bring

about a change in 'history', but it does this through individual lives and their response to God's approach. We noted that many of the twenty-five sayings either actually stress or else clearly imply some element of human acceptance of God's plan of action or even identification with it, and any action which is characterised by personal acceptance and commitment must be in some degree psychological. If by saying that the kingdom is not psychological is meant that individuals and their attitudes are of no importance and are just over-ruled, then it is simply not true of what Jesus taught about the kingdom.

God's Kingdom is effective in history because it is first of all effective in the lives of individuals whose lives are changed into something which God can use in his further work.

To pray, therefore 'Your Kingdom come' means that we earnestly desire that God will take full control—of our own personal lives, of the society within which we live, of the whole world of which we are a part. When God takes control he both brings his salvation and also requires full obedience. That obedience may demand heavy sacrifices, but in return there comes an experience of life at its richest and most rewarding. This Reign of God is something which men may taste and rejoice in here and now; in the future it will bring to mankind something far better than anything they have known in the present or in the past; it is a future which embraces not only this earthly life but also life beyond death. It is God's future for his people. It is this for whose coming Christians have prayed and still do pray.

4. SOME INTERPRETERS OF THE KINGDOM: THE SYNOPTIC GOSPELS

1. MATTHEW

We have examined those sayings of Jesus about the kingdom which appear to have the strongest claim to authenticity. We must now look at the sayings attributed to him which have been subjected to editorial modification. We turn first to those found in Matthew's gospel. Our aim will be to discover those aspects of the kingdom as Jesus proclaimed it which Matthew felt should be given special emphasis, and also those aspects which appear to have been imposed by Matthew on to sayings which did not originally contain them.

We have noted that more than any other of the evangelists Matthew wished to give prominence to the idea of the kingdom. He records forty-six sayings of Jesus about the kingdom, as compared with thirty-one in Luke and fourteen in Mark. Some of Matthew's forty-six occur also in Mark or Luke or both, but twenty-seven are peculiar to Matthew's gospel. The larger number of such sayings in Matthew as compared with Luke and Mark would of itself awaken a suspicion that he may have introduced the idea of the kingdom into some contexts where it had not originally been found, and closer examination does in fact confirm this.

We have already noted in Matthew's gospel a tendency to select a comparatively rare feature in Mark and exaggerate it so as to make it appear as a dominant aspect of the teaching of Jesus. The word 'hypocrite', for instance, applied to Pharisees, occurs only once in Mark; in Matthew it appears fourteen times. One assumes that Matthew himself had come to feel a bitter resentment against this feature of Pharisaic Judaism and allowed his own hostility to be read back into the teaching of Jesus by exaggerating the frequency with which Jesus spoke of Pharisees as 'hypocrites'. Similarly the phrase about 'weeping and gnashing', which appears only once in Mark, occurs five times in Matthew, introducing a note of vindictiveness towards the enemies of Christ. Again, the word 'fulfil' is one of which Matthew is exceedingly fond, especially as applied to Old Testament prophecies. This idea of 'fulfilment' was no doubt a feature of the earliest forms of Christianity, since it is found twice in Mark and twice in Luke. But Matthew clearly heightens the effect by introducing it in no less than fourteen contexts. This idea of the Christian faith as a fulfilment of hopes and expectations in the Jewish past was clearly a very important part of Matthew's thinking. Further the word 'righteousness', which does not occur at all in Mark, and is found only once in Luke, appears seven times in Matthew. This suggests that for Matthew 'righteousness' also was a very important matter. Matthew also has far more references to future rewards and punishments associated with the end of time than the other two synoptists. One scholar represented this numerically by estimating that Mark had five such references, Luke also five, and Matthew forty-four. Even if this is not a precisely accurate count the very wide differences indicates that for Matthew the subject loomed very large. The presence in Matthew of significant words which are totally absent from the other evangelists is also worth noting, words such as *parousia*, *ekklesia*, '*palingenesia*' (translated in N.E.B. as 'the world that is to be'), and the phrase 'the consummation of the age'. Three of these show a preoccupation with an apocalyptic view of the future.

Features such as these, which make Matthew notably different from the other synoptists in certain aspects of his outlook, put us on the alert to detect similar divergencies in his attitude to the kingdom; and indeed we do find that there are in Matthew three distinctive emphases in his presentation of the teaching of Jesus about the kingdom. They are: his somewhat artificial association of the kingdom with parables which originally had no such precise link; his introduction of the idea of 'righteousness' into sayings about the kingdom, and a heightening of the apocalyptic element.

a The Parables

There is no doubt that in the teaching of Jesus some of the parables are specifically linked with the idea of the kingdom. At Mk. 4.30 the parable of the mustard seed is introduced by two parallel questions (a device characteristic of Jesus): 'With what can we compare the Kingdom of God? or what parable (analogy) shall we use for it?' Also at Lk. 13.20 a similar question introduces the parable of the leaven. There is little doubt that the linking of these two parables with the message of the kingdom is part of the authentic teaching of Jesus.

Sometimes the link between the parable and the kingdom does not depend on some precise feature in the parable (like a seed or leaven) but on the action of the parable as a whole. For instance, at Mk. 4.26 the kingdom is not likened precisely to the *man* who sowed, but rather to the whole parable: 'The Kingdom of God is *as if* a man sowed ...'.

It is the action in the whole parable which contains the parallel: there is sowing and harvesting, but the parallel to the kingdom is not the man who sows and reaps, but the whole mysterious process of germination, growth and fruitfulness. This is God's marvellous gift to man, a gift which man can only accept with wonder, since he himself can neither understand it nor reproduce it. So it is with the kingdom ... a man may under God proclaim the reality of the kingdom, and may be able to rejoice in the outcome when men open their lives and receive the kingdom, yet that which enables a man to receive the proclamation and respond fruitfully to it is 'all God's doing' (as Paul said in a similar context in 2 Cor. 5.18), and is marvellous in our eyes (see Mk. 12.11).

These three parables are spoken to portray some aspect of the kingdom, and probably other parables had the same purpose. Matthew certainly thought so and prefaced many parables with a standard formula of introduction: 'The Kingdom of heaven is like ...', even though originally the parable probably was told without any precise link with the kingdom. Sometimes his interpretation of a parable in this way may point to its original meaning, but sometimes it is misleading. For instance, the two parables about the treasure in the

71

field and the pearl of great price very probably were spoken by Jesus to illustrate and enforce some truth about the kingdom. It is, however, doubtful whether Jesus was responsible for the form of the introductory words: 'The Kingdom of heaven is like a treasure ...'. The thrust of the parable is not really about the treasure waiting in the ground till some diligent person unearths it. What we are pointed to in the parable is the attitude of the man who finds the treasure and wants it with such intensity that he is willing to give up everything else if only that will enable him to gain it. So too with the parable about the pearl. Yet, oddly enough, this parable, though using the same introductory formula, compares the kingdom not with the pearl but—even more unsuitably—the merchant. In fact both parables are about the right way to respond when a man finds himself confronted with the kingdom, and not really about the kingdom being like a treasure or a pearl, though one can see the attractiveness in such an interpretation.

Similarly this introductory formula, rather awkwardly attached to some others of Matthew's parables, is plainly unsuitable. The Kingdom of God is *not* like a man sowing seed (13.24), nor is it like a king (18.23 and 22.1), nor like *ten virgins* (25.1). Some of these parables may be underlining some truth related to the kingdom, but it is the story as a whole which reveals the truth, not the single figure to which the introductory formula links it. A better introduction would have been: 'Here is another picture of the Kingdom', as the N.E.B. takes the liberty of translating the formula at Mt. 13.45. The likeness to the kingdom lies in the whole story rather than in one feature or person in it.

It would therefore be quite misleading to expound these parables exactly as Matthew reports them, and then to say that this is the teaching of Jesus. The parable itself probably is the teaching of Jesus, but not the introductory formula with which Matthew artificially related it to the kingdom. Moreover in some of these parables there is an apocalyptic interpretation included which, as we have seen, is much more characteristic of Matthew's own theological emphasis than of the teaching about the kingdom by Jesus himself. Each parable needs to be considered on its own, without assuming that Matthew's interpretation of it can be identified with that of Jesus.

b Righteousness

We have already noted that in the gospel of Matthew as a whole the word 'righteousness' is a favourite one with the author. Mark does not use it at all, and Luke only once (and that in the early Christian hymn we call the Benedictus, Luke 1.74). Matthew, however, uses it seven times and several of these are connected with the kingdom. Indeed it has been claimed that Matthew regarded it as a kind of simplified interpretation of what the kingdom means. Certainly in 6.33 the words appear as synonyms. Luke, in the parallel passage (Lk. 12.31) has simply: 'Seek God's Kingdom ...'. Matthew, however, amplifies this into 'Seek first his Kingdom *and his righteousness*'. Further in Mt. 5.10 it is those who endure persecution 'for the sake of righteousness' who possess the kingdom, and at 5.20 only those enter the kingdom whose 'righteousness' is better than that of the scribes and Pharisees (that is, with a personal commitment to the will of God far more discerning and sincere than is involved in a mere external obedience to a set of rules). In similar vein it is the 'righteous' who will shine as the sun in the Kingdom of the Father (13.43); and in contrast all doers of 'lawlessness' are excluded from the kingdom (13.41).

Matthew clearly wished to emphasise the moral content of the Kingdom of God. 'Righteousness', when given its true meaning, was an integral part of the kingdom, and he made sure his readers would understand this. Another way in which he sought to ensure the same end was by showing how obedience to the will of God (that is, true righteousness) was an essential part of the kingdom. In the Lord's Prayer, for instance, Luke has simply: 'Your Kingdom come', but Matthew adds a parallel, interpretative clause: 'Your will be done on earth as it is in heaven'. So it can be said that he saw both 'righteousness' and 'doing the will of God' as rough equivalents to the kingdom. Similarly in Mt. 7.21 it is not verbal protests of loyalty and devotion which gain a person's access into the kingdom, but actually 'doing God's will'.

Although Jesus himself may have avoided the use of the word 'righteousness', there is little doubt that emphasis on 'doing the will of God' was an authentic part of his teaching. It controlled his own life and ought to control that of his followers. His avoidance of the word 'righteousness' may be due to the fact that in conventional religious usage it had come to mean little more than formal obedience to certain prescribed rules of conduct. Matthew in adopting it may even have fostered some of the wrong thinking which Jesus had deliberately sought to avoid. There can be little doubt that for Jesus the Kingdom of God meant not observance of prescribed rules but a personal relationship to God as Father and total obedience to him as a known and loved person. To live in the kingdom meant an earnest intention to do his will. But it was God who brought the kingdom and established it in human lives. Men and women could accept or decline God's offered rule in their lives. Their obedience, however, was man's proper response to God's coming, not a device by which men could establish the Kingdom of God by their own efforts. It is most unlikely that Jesus ever spoke of righteousness as a kind of ladder by which men could climb into the Kingdom of God or as a device by which that kingdom could be established on earth. Yet some of the words attributed to Jesus by Matthew may give that impression. Matthew sometimes makes it appear as if human righteousness is a prerequisite of the coming of the kingdom. This, however, is Pharisaic teaching rather than the proclamation of the gospel. For Jesus righteousness is the consequence of God's coming in his kingdom.

Matthew was clearly wishing to make clear beyond any doubt that righteousness, as properly understood, is an indispensable part of the Kingdom of God. It is more than likely that what gave him this concern was the presence in the churches he knew of an element which tended to regard salvation or participation in God's Kingdom as little more than an inward experience of spiritual renewal and ecstatic happiness. Emphasis on moral conduct and obligations was dismissed as a relapse into legalism rather than the gospel.

God forgives all through Christ; human righteousness is only human pride in a moral garb. Such an attitude led to a disregard for moral goodness and a lack of urgent concern for integrity and justice. God's grace was made 'cheap', in that man accepts it gratefully but makes no attempt to make a return which God looks for. Matthew saw this attitude to be utterly wrong, but in setting himself to counter it he seems sometimes to have allowed himself to represent righteousness, so that it appears, not only as an indispensable consequence of God's Kingdom in human life and society, but also as a kind of necessary preliminary to it.

We may therefore regret that some of Matthew's words seem to support a one-sided moralistic form of Christianity, as when he writes in 21.43 that the kingdom is to be given to the nation which produces its fruits. But we can appreciate the dangerous threat to the Church in the deviation he was trying to correct, and welcome his determination to insist that true righteousness, understood as doing the will of God as made known through Jesus, is an inescapable concomitant of the kingdom.

Matthew, however, does not always keep the meaning of righteousness at its highest level. Some of his uses of it seem dangerously near to a kind of Christian legalism. But he is right to insist on the moral content of the Kingdom of God and righteousness is one of the words he chose to use to achieve this end. By means of it he insisted that the Kingdom of God was more than emotional ecstasy; but he may have opened the door to the opposite danger of so stressing the moral implications of the kingdom as to diminish its spiritual base in a right relationship with God. So too today the kingdom has sometimes been equated with the achievement of justice (righteousness) in human affairs. It is true that the kingdom will produce men and women whose hearts are set on justice, but the determination to remedy injustice is not in itself identical with the kingdom.

Those, however, who tend to think of the Kingdom of God as a private, merely individual experience need the strong reminders of Matthew that, where the Kingdom of God is, there is to be found not only an experience of the God who heals our personal unhappiness, but an awareness also that this God is one who commands our obedience, and this means uprightness of personal conduct and in the community a concern for justice and the welfare of others. And this is the meaning of righteousness.

3 Apocalyptic

We have noted how references to resurrection, future rewards and punishments and the coming of the Son of Man in glory occur far more frequently in Matthew than in Luke and Mark. It is not surprising therefore to find that some of these 'eschatological' references are associated with the kingdom. These are sometimes found in material which is peculiar to Matthew, sometimes in the changed wording which Matthew introduces into sayings which are reported also in Mark or Luke.

We look especially at those sayings which are of an apocalyptic nature, where the coming of the kingdom is associated with the coming of the Son of Man in glory, where the kingdom is represented as a supernatural intervention by God in human affairs. We will examine these and ask how far they may be regarded as genuine sayings of Jesus or how far they should be treated as editorial redactions by Matthew. It is important that this should be done because ever since Schweitzer first made the claim other scholars have continued to repeat it—that in the mind of Jesus the coming of the kingdom and the coming of the Son of Man were identified as in effect the same event. Our contention is that the evidence does not support this, and that it was not Jesus but such Christian writers as Matthew who gave to the kingdom this apocalyptic dimension.

We have had occasion elsewhere to comment on Mt. 16.28 where Matthew is reproducing the material of Mk. 9.1 where Jesus speaks of some contemporaries who will live to 'see the Kingdom of God having come with power'. Matthew introduces an apocalyptic note into it by changing Mark's words to: '... see the Son of Man coming in his Kingdom'. The introduction of the Son of Man at this point is wholly the work of Matthew.

Kingdom and Son of Man are also associated in Mt. 13.41, a passage found only in Matthew. It comes in the explanation of the parable of the tares where Jesus is reported as saying: 'The Son of Man will send his angels and will gather out of his kingdom all causes of sin and all evildoers'. Then the righteous will shine like the sun in the Kingdom of their Father. We note that the kingdom here is referred to not only as the Kingdom of God ('of their Father') but also as the Kingdom of Christ ('Son of Man'). This is a feature characteristic of Matthew rather than Jesus. Moreover scholars are almost unanimous in regarding the occasional explanation attached to parables as coming from the post-resurrection Church rather than from Jesus himself.

Again in Mt. 24.10–14 (which has no parallel in Mark or Luke) the coming of the kingdom is given an apocalyptic setting. The signs which herald 'the end' are listed—persecution, disruption of the Christian community, false prophets, increase of wickedness, the fading of Christian devotion. But in spite of all discouragement 'the gospel of the kingdom' will be proclaimed over the whole world, and only then will the end come. These words also are much more likely to reflect the thoughts of Matthew than those of Jesus, who firmly discouraged those who asked for signs of what was going to happen.

Similarly in Mk. 10.35 the brothers James and John ask Jesus to promise them places of special privilege 'in your glory'. Matthew in 20.21 makes two significant changes in this wording. The first is that he discreetly represents the request as coming from the mother of the two disciples and not from the disciples themselves—but this is not significant for our present discussion. The second is that he changes 'in your glory' to 'in your Kingdom'. Whatever Mark meant by Christ's glory', Matthew interprets as meaning the coming of the Son of Man in his Kingdom. By the same change Matthew has once again, whether intentionally or not, made the words speak of the Kingdom as Christ's rather than God's. This is characteristic of Matthew.

Another saying with an apocalyptic flavour is Mt. 21.43: 'The Kingdom of God will be taken away from you and given to a nation reproducing the fruit of it'. It is added by Matthew to material which he has been following from Mk. 12.1–12. Luke, however, when he reproduces this same passage from Mark, has no equivalent to Mt. 21.43. So these words are peculiar to Matthew only. It speaks of the kingdom being removed from those who felt themselves entitled to it, and bestowed on others who were counted more worthy. The content of the saying is not unlike the saying reported in Mt. 8.12 and Lk. 13.28–29, which declares that foreigners from east and west will take their place in the kingdom whereas the 'sons of the Kingdom' (Luke has 'you') will be excluded. Moreover the fact that Matthew uses here the phrase 'Kingdom of God' (instead of Kingdom of heaven) which is contrary to his usual practice suggests that he received this saying from the tradition and did not just formulate it himself. It may therefore be that the saying embodies pre-Matthaean traditional material. The particular form in which Matthew quotes it, however, reflects Matthaean attitudes. Some have felt that it suggests that the kingdom is awarded to those who deserve it most, which is not an emphasis associated with Jesus.

The evidence suggests that Matthew paraphrased the teaching of Jesus about the kingdom so as to make it clear that in his judgement it was apocalyptic. Some, however, argue that this element was already present in what Jesus taught and Matthew merely gave it heightened emphasis because to him it seemed very important (just as he gave an exaggerated frequency to the use of the word 'hypocrite'). What, however, is clear is that in Matthew this element receives far greater prominence than it had in the actual teaching of Jesus.

Why he did this we can only speculate. Perhaps he lived at a time when the expectation of the Parousia was fading. But Matthew understood Jesus to have foretold that it would happen within the lifetime of some of his disciples. If so, it must take place very soon. It was his duty to place such emphasis on it that people would be alerted to its nearness, and so to inject a new sense of urgency in the proclamation of the Gospel.

It seems most unlikely that Jesus himself spoke about his

Second Coming or even outlined the signs and sufferings which would herald it. The supposed preludes to the Day of the Lord were familiar within Judaism. Much more likely to be authentic are the words of Jesus warning his disciples not to speculate about the future; and not to look for signs: 'No sign shall be given to them'; 'It is not for you to know times or seasons . . .'; 'Of that day not even the Son knows, only the Father'. There is little doubt that Jesus anticipated his own early death and the apparent failure of his mission. There would be nothing specially supernatural about such insight. Martin Luther King had the same sense of destiny. It is likely also that Jesus spoke of a great ultimate victory of all he stood for in God's future, and believed that the way of suffering he was asked to take was something which God would use in achieving that final victory. But it is most unlikely that he tried to specify when this would be, or suggest signs that would warn of its nearness. Matthew was right in his certainty that God's cause would prevail; it is clear that he was not right in the way he chose to try to enforce this truth upon his contemporaries, since what he foretold in the near future did not take place.

2. LUKE

Luke is a less forceful editor than Matthew. He is more hesitant about making changes in the material which he has accepted as suitable for incorporation into his gospel. Compared with Matthew there are fewer instances where he can be seen making significant alterations in it. This does not mean that Luke's gospel does not have marked characteristics, as Matthew's does, but these appear more in his selection of material from what is available to him than in his adaptation of what he selects. When the same references to the kingdom in Luke and Matthew are compared it is Luke who usually prefers to retain the words in the same form as they have come to him, whereas Matthew introduces significant alterations. Some instances of this are as follows:

Luke 6.20	Matthew 5.3
Blessed are you poor, for yours is the Kingdom of God.	Blessed are the poor *in spirit*, for theirs is the Kingdom of heaven.

Luke 11.2	Matthew 6.10
Your Kingdom come.	Your Kingdom come; *your will be done* on earth as it is in heaven.

Luke 12.31	Matthew 6.33
Seek his Kingdom and these things shall be yours as well.	Seek first his Kingdom *and his righteousness* and all these things shall be yours as well.

Luke 9.27 (cf. Mk. 9.1)	Matthew 16.28
There are some standing here who will not taste death before they see the Kingdom of God.	There are some standing here who will not taste death before they see *the Son of Man coming* in his Kingdom.

Luke 8.12 (cf. Mk. 9.34)	Matthew 13.19
The ones along the path are those who have heard ...	When anyone hears the word *of the Kingdom* ...

Luke 9.46 (cf. Mk. 9.34)	Matthew 18.1
An argument arose among them about which of them was greatest.	At that time the disciples came to Jesus saying: 'Who is greatest *in the Kingdom of heaven*?'

In all these cases Luke's version appears to be nearer to the original without any particularly Lucan feature added.

At one or two places, however, Luke does allow his own beliefs to affect the way he reports sayings about the kingdom. One is the frequency with which he represents the Kingdom of God as the theme of the preaching both of

Jesus and his disciples. Mark does not do this. He says that they preached that the kingdom was near, but he does not say that they preached the kingdom, as if the kingdom were a compendium of theology. Luke, however, does speak of Jesus as 'preaching the Kingdom', for example in 8.1 (where he uses both of the two Greek words for preaching: *kēryssō* and *euangelizomai*) and of the disciples doing so in 9.2 (*kēryssō*). Sometimes he adds this feature to Markan material, where it is not present in Mark. For instance, in Mark 1.38 we read that Jesus said: 'Let us go on to the next towns that I may preach there also'. In the same context in Luke (Lk. 4.43) it is: 'I must preach *the good news of the Kingdom of God* to the other cities also'. Sometimes also, as compared with Matthew, the kingdom as the theme of preaching is introduced by Luke. Mt. 11.13 has: 'For all the prophets and the law prophesied until John' (with no reference to preaching), whereas Luke 16.16 has: 'The law and the prophets were until John; since then the good news of the Kingdom is preached (*euangelizomai*). At Lk. 9.60 and Mt. 8.22 the hesitant disciple is told to 'leave the dead to bury their dead', but only in Luke are the further words added: 'Go and proclaim (*diangellō*) the Kingdom of God'.

Matthew also, in fact, writes of the kingdom as the subject for preaching, though less frequently than Luke. For Mark, however, the kingdom is not thought of as the subject for a sermon, but rather as God's urgent approach to man to which man must be called to respond with equal urgency. For Luke, however, it seems as though the gospel and the kingdom and the kerygma were largely identified.

Luke also on one occasion associates the coming of the kingdom with the coming of the Son of Man, though in a different context from that of Matthew. This is at Lk. 21.31. He is following fairly closely the apocalyptic passages from Mark 13, and naming the signs which will be the prelude to *the coming of the Son of Man*. He reproduces from Mark the parable of the fig tree (Mk. 13.28) which in the Markan context is related to the signs of the coming of the Son of Man (as it is also in Mt. 24.33). But Luke alters this and instead inserts the idea that these signs are an indication that '*the Kingdom of God*' is near. The introduction of the kingdom at this point and in relation to the Son of Man has therefore been imposed on his material, because in this respect he differs not only from Mark but also from Matthew's reproduction of Mark.

Luke also refers to the coming of the kingdom as a future, and apparently, an apocalyptic event in 22.18. There Jesus says: 'I will not drink of the fruit of the vine until the Kingdom of God *comes*'. In the same context, in both Mark and Matthew, Jesus says that he will not drink again of the fruit of the vine until he 'drinks it new in the Kingdom of God', a phrasing which does not carry any distinctly apocalyptic meaning. But Luke inserts the idea of the 'coming' of the kingdom.

In these last two contexts the reference to the kingdom appears to be to a future apocalyptic event, but this significance has been imposed by Luke on material which did not originally contain it.

Another feature which begins to appear in Luke, but is not found in Mark is that the kingdom is spoken of as the Kingdom of Christ, rather than of God. At Luke 22.29 Jesus speaks of his disciples as eating and drinking 'at my table in my Kingdom'. In the parallel saying in Mt. 19.22 there is no reference at all to the kingdom. So too at Lk. 23.42 the dying thief speaks of Jesus 'coming in his Kingdom'.

This feature is present also in Matthew. At Mt. 20.21 two disciples speaking to Jesus refer to the kingdom as 'your Kingdom' and at Mt. 13.41 the kingdom is the Kingdom of the Son of Man. This tendency to speak of the kingdom as 'Christ's' seems to be characteristic of a later development in the Church. It is found also in Jn. 18.36, Col. 1.13, Eph. 5.5, 2 Tim. 4.1, 4.18, 2 Pet. 1.11, Rev. 11.15.

Another tendency as time went on was for Christians to substitute the person of Christ for the kingdom. At Mark 10.29 Jesus speaks of disciples who abandon family and possessions 'for my sake and for the sake of the Gospel'. In Mt. 19.29 they do so 'for my name's sake'. Luke 18.29, on the other hand, prefers 'for the sake of the Kingdom of God', even though he appears to be reproducing from Mark. Is it that in this instance Luke is giving preference to an earlier mode of expression?

There is therefore less to be said about Luke's redactional activity with regard to the kingdom than of Matthew's. But we do note his emphasis on 'preaching the Kingdom of God', his awareness that in the life of the Church the coming of the kingdom was being identified with the coming of the Son of Man, and his occasional use of a phrase to modify an earlier reference to the Kingdom of God so that it becomes the Kingdom of Christ.

3. MARK

It is much more difficult to detect in Mark any personal interpretations of sayings about the Kingdom of God, because we have no earlier form of the tradition with which to compare him. In the case of Matthew and Luke we can compare their form of the sayings with what they found in Mark, and we can also compare them with one another. But there is nothing similar by which we can check Mark. In almost every case where Matthew and Luke alter a saying which they have found in Mark, their modifications take the saying further from its original form. The only exception appeared to be Lk. 18.29, where the phrase 'for the sake of the Kingdom of God' may represent an earlier form of the tradition than that contained in Mark's 'for my sake' (Mk. 10.29).

All the sayings of Jesus about the kingdom which are found in Mark were regarded as worthy to be included in the twenty-five with the greatest claim to authenticity. The reference to Joseph of Arimathea as one who was 'waiting for the Kingdom of God' was not included because it is not a saying attributed to Jesus. We even included Mk. 4.22 with its reference to 'the mystery of the Kingdom' because it is substantially reproduced—and therefore approved—by both Matthew and Luke as well as Mark, but in our judgement this phrase belongs rather to Mark as editor than to Jesus. Even if the phrase itself is traced back to Jesus, it is most improbable that in his teaching it was associated with parables. This description of the parables as problem pieces is much more likely to represent Mark's point of view than that of

Jesus. According to Mark 4.30 Jesus uses parables to help clarify his meaning.

The most important comment to make on Mark's sayings about the kingdom is a negative rather than a positive one. It is this: that though Mark clearly accepted the belief current in the early Church that the Son of Man would soon return in glory (Mk. 13.26), he does not allow this personal belief to affect the way he reports the sayings about the kingdom (as we have seen both Matthew and Luke do on occasion). In Mark the coming of the Kingdom of God is never identified with or even associated with the coming of the Son of Man. In this respect we believe that Mark truly reproduces the authentic note of the sayings of Jesus. In Matthew and Luke there is the danger that the Kingdom of God becomes a rigid circumscribed concept identified with one particular event in the future. In Mark it is a much more flexible idea, as flexible indeed as that of the will of God, with an important bearing not only on one event in the future, but on every individual Christian and on every moment of history.

4. SYNONYMS OF THE KINGDOM IN THE SYNOPTICS

Before concluding our examination of the meaning of the Kingdom of God in the synoptic gospels, we should recognise that, on occasions, what the kingdom stands for can be expressed in other words. We noted earlier that Matthew used the word 'righteousness' to describe the content of the kingdom, sometimes using it almost as a synonym.

Matthew also is aware that the phrase 'the spirit of God' shares a large area of common meaning with 'the Kingdom of God'. At Mt. 12.28, for instance, he records that Jesus said: 'If I by *the Spirit of God* cast out demons, then has the *Kingdom of God* come upon you'. It is true that at Lk. 11.20 Luke, in reporting the same saying, uses, instead of 'the Spirit of God', the more anthropomorphic phrase 'the finger of God'. It is odd that in this variation of wording it is Matthew who has Spirit where Luke uses another word, because of the three synoptists it is Luke who gives most prominence to the Spirit of God. But even if Jesus did originally use 'finger' and not 'Spirit', the meaning—for non-Jewish readers at any rate—is better expressed by 'Spirit'. The Spirit of God symbolises that of God which is powerfully and effectively active in human life, and this is something very close to what is meant by the Kingdom of God. In this context, certainly, the Spirit of God is the effective agent of the Kingdom of God.

With this clue to guide us we can recognise in other areas also a close relationship between Spirit and Kingdom. The new accession of spiritual insight and power which came to Jesus at his baptism is described in terms of the Holy Spirit coming upon him, and in that power he was able to announce the arrival of the Kingdom of God. Equally one could express the significance of what happened to Jesus at the baptism by saying that God was investing him with those powers which would equip him to be an effective agent of the Kingdom of God. The interesting variant of the prayer 'Your Kingdom come' in Lk. 11.2 similarly uses God's Spirit as an equivalent of the Kingdom: May your Holy Spirit come upon us.

Synonyms for the Spirit of God also appear in such words as 'fire' and 'power'. In Mt. 3.11 John the Baptist promises about Jesus: He will baptise you with the Holy Spirit and fire. It is more than likely that the original form of the saying spoke only of baptising with *fire*, and the Spirit was added later to suggest what 'fire' meant. This recalls Lk. 12.49 where Jesus said: 'I came to cast fire on the earth, and how I wish it was already kindled'. This is in effect an expression of the longing Jesus felt for the in-breaking of the life and vitality of God's Kingdom. Luke also both in the gospel and Acts, closely identified 'power' with the Holy Spirit (e.g., Lk. 24.49). In consequence, 'fire' and 'power', as well as the Spirit of God or the Holy Spirit, may be regarded as lying within the same complex of ideas as the Kingdom of God.

Another word which in certain contexts appears to be used as a kind of synonym of the kingdom—or at least as a synonym for part of the total significance of the kingdom—is 'Life'. Jesus spoke of 'life' as existing at two levels—a lower level which one must be prepared to turn one's back on, and a higher level which may be gained by such renunciation: 'Whoever seeks to gain his life will lose it, but whoever loses his life will preserve it' (Lk. 17.33). It is this fuller life which may be used as an equivalent of the kingdom, and the lower level, which may need to be sacrificed for it, consists of the material and physical to which we can be excessively attached. In Mk. 9.43–47 there is a saying of Jesus which falls into the threefold pattern he used so often: If your hand, or your foot, or your eye causes you to stumble, get rid of it; for it is better to go into life maimed than with all your faculties to go into Gehenna. In the first two of the three divisions (concerning hand and foot) the gain to be grasped as 'life'; in the third the wording is changed to 'Kingdom of God'. Clearly 'life' and 'Kingdom' are used as equivalents, or at least as partial equivalents. This means that the effect of the coming of the kingdom into the experience of the disciple may fairly be described as 'life'. That is, where God is allowed full control of human personality, that personality comes to Life, gains authentic Life.

The approximate equivalence between 'Life' and 'Kingdom' is found also in Mk. 10.17–23 (and its parallel in Mt. 19.16–23). A young man asks Jesus: 'What must I do to gain eternal *life*?'. Jesus suggests what the man should do, only to find his counsel rejected, and comments: 'How hard it is for those who have riches to enter the *Kingdom of God*'. 'Eternal life' and the 'Kingdom' appear in this passage to mean much the same. Similarly at Lk. 12.15 Jesus insists that 'a man's real life (*zoē*) does not come from his possessions', and at Lk. 12.31 adds: 'Seek the Kingdom of God and these things (material requirements) will be added'. 'Life' and 'Kingdom' both describe the eternal realities which men should set their hearts on. We shall need to look further at this use of 'life' when we consider the fourth gospel in which 'eternal life' seems almost to be accepted as the regular substitute for what in the synoptic gospels appears as the Kingdom of God.

It would, however, be misleading to think of 'life' as a *complete* synonym for kingdom. It is only certain elements in the kingdom which would be described as life, and life would

86

be used only where it these elements which predominate. The kingdom, however, in its totality has wider implications than life. Righteousness and the Holy Spirit point to other dimensions of the kingdom not wholly covered by life.

5. OTHER INTERPRETERS OF THE KINGDOM OF GOD

1. JOHN

There are many features of the fourth gospel which distinguish it from the synoptics. One of them is that in the synoptics the phrase 'The Kingdom of God' (or Heaven) is the constantly recurring theme in the teaching of Jesus. Matthew reports it forty-six times on the lips of Jesus, Luke thirty-one, and Mark fourteen. In contrast to this, in the fourth gospel the phrase appears only twice, and both of these occur in the same episode and within the space of three verses. For some reason John preferred to avoid the phrase, and it appears more than likely that when he does allow himself to introduce it it is to correct certain misuses of it which he regards as misleading.

The context in which the phrase is found is the conversation between Jesus and Nicodemus in chapter 3.1–12, an incident which has certain similarities to that of the 'rich young ruler' in Lk. 18.18–25. Some indeed have argued that the same historical encounter lies behind both passages. The Nicodemus incident opens with some words of courtesy from the enquirer: 'We know you are a teacher come from God; for no one can do these signs that you do, unless God is with him'. The reply of Jesus is quite unrelated to this, and seems to plunge without warning into a topic the reader is quite unprepared for: 'Truly, truly, I say to you, unless one is born anew he cannot see the Kingdom of God'. One has the impression that the reported conversation has been greatly abbreviated, and that a question from Nicodemus has been omitted, perhaps a request to be told how a man may enter or gain a place in the Kingdom of God. Certainly at Lk. 18.18 the enquirer (described there as a 'ruler' as Nicodemus also is described in Jn. 3.1) raises a question: 'What shall I do to inherit eternal life?' A similar question would prepare the way for John 3.3 where Jesus in answer speaks of the need to be born anew in order to 'see' the Kingdom of God. In verse 5 the word 'see' is changed to 'enter'. It may be that the two words are meant as variants without any difference of meaning being intended. If, however, the variation is intentional and significant, then in verse 3 the reply of Jesus means: 'You are asking about entering the Kingdom. A man does not even become aware of the kingdom until God has worked in him an inward change, so basic as to be called being begotten or being born "anew".' The unmistakable emphasis in the words is that the kingdom is not something which men can achieve by good intentions and shrewd planning. It becomes possible for him only if a fundamental change is brought about in his inner life, a change which only God can work. The word here translated 'anew' in the original Greek may have two meanings. One is 'again', 'a second time'; the other is 'from above', that is 'from God'. Nicodemus understands it only in the first sense, because he speaks, a little sarcastically perhaps, of entering the womb 'a second time'. But the meaning Jesus really intended is 'from above', that is a radical inward change must first be brought about in the man by God.

This double meaning of the Greek word is apparently an ambiguity which is not found in any corresponding Aramaic word. Since Jesus spoke in Aramaic, the conclusion has been drawn that this cannot be regarded as an authentic saying of the historical Jesus, but one which has taken its present shape in a Greek-speaking world. This is probably true. But it could well be that the essential meaning behind the saying does go back to Jesus himself. At any rate words with a similar emphasis are attributed to him in the synoptic gospels. For instance, at Mt. 12.33 Jesus said: 'Either make the tree good and its fruit good, or make the tree bad and its fruit bad', which implies that a new kind of person is required if this new way of life is to be followed. The presence of the characteristic word of Jesus at the beginning of the statement in Jn. 3.3, 'Truly', suggests that John felt he was accurately representing what Jesus had said.

The reply of Jesus to Nicodemus's somewhat pedestrian irony is: 'Unless one is born of the water and the Spirit he cannot enter the Kingdom of God'. What is implied in being born 'anew' is spelt out more fully. The Spirit is the power or presence of God active in human life. God's presence within the human life must bring about a radical change before the Kingdom of God becomes a reality for a man. The double emphasis is clear. To have a place in God's Kingdom there must be an inward transformation of a man's life, and that change can be achieved only by the Spirit of God. It is all God's doing, as Paul himself insists in a similar passage in 2 Cor. 5.18. The Kingdom of God is a real life-changing experience of the individual believer—not some external event for which he waits and hopes.

It is emphasised that man cannot organise or control this process. It is the work of God's Spirit, and that Spirit is like the wind whose movements man can neither predict nor determine nor control. So the re-birth of the human spirit at the touch of God is something man cannot predict or determine. When it happens, man cannot explain why it should happen now and not then, or here and not there, to one and not to another. There is a mystery about spiritual awakenings in the presence of which man can only be humble and grateful.

John is not alone in associating the need for rebirth with the Kingdom of God. Matthew at 18.3 does the same. In reproducing the Markan saying: 'Whoever does not receive the Kingdom of God as a child, will not enter into it', he introduces the insistence on rebirth, and makes it more directly personal: 'Unless *you* turn and become like little children you cannot enter the Kingdom of heaven'. The A.V. translated this: 'Except ye be converted . . .', an equivalent of 'rebirth'.

In Luke 18.18 the ruler asks Jesus how he may gain *eternal life*, and is told that a rich man cannot enter *the Kingdom of God*. In a similar way but in the reverse order in John 3 it is the Kingdom of God which is first introduced, to be followed in 3.15 by an explanation about eternal life. At other places in the synoptics we noted that 'life' could be used as a synonym for the kingdom. For John this has become his normal practice. In this passage, however, the only one where he uses the phrase 'the Kingdom of God', he introduces it to emphasise certain aspects of the Kingdom which he felt to be important—that it was not to be thought of as some outward event in which man could be externally involved as a spectator, but an intensely personal matter which needs a radical, inward rebirth of his own life, changing it from something inauthentic to what was truly authentic, to use the modern phraseology. This emphasis had been present in the original teaching of Jesus about the kingdom, but in John's time apparently it was being replaced by an understanding of the kingdom which was much more external to the man himself, like some future cataclysm. So John's own emphasis here is that God's rule in human life can begin NOW; and when it does begin it brings a man's life to a new birth which produces true life or as Jn. 10.10 calls it, 'abundant life', authentic life; and this rebirth and the new life that follows is wholly the work of God.

We have not considered the word 'water' in Jn. 3.5: 'Unless one is born of the water and the Spirit, he cannot enter the Kingdom of God'. The word does not seem to make any clear contribution to the understanding of the kingdom. Commentators have not been able to agree on its meaning, but the verse in its completeness is clearly insisting that no substitute can be found for the work of God's Spirit in bringing about a real spiritual change in the man. Certainly nothing that man can do or arrange suffices to produce this rebirth. It is wholly God's doing, and it is so essential that nothing can be regarded as a substitute for it—neither a sacramental ritual nor a self-directed moral reformation.

Although the actual phrase 'The Kingdom of God' occurs only twice in the fourth gospel, there are three instances where Jesus is represented as speaking of 'my kingdom'. All three occur within one single verse, Jn. 18.36: 'Jesus answered: My kingdom is not of this world; if my kingdom were of this world, my servants would fight, that I might not be handed over to the Jews; but my kingdom is not from this world'. (R.S.V. actually in this sentence translated 'kingdom' as 'kingship'.)

Perhaps in this verse we see another reason why the phrase

'the Kingdom of God' was avoided by John. It could so easily be misunderstood and misrepresented as having political, even nationalist, connotations, which would arouse the suspicions of Roman authorities. Since, however, the word kingdom had its place firmly in the tradition of the teaching of Jesus, John seeks to divest it of elements which might give offence. He does this in three ways: (1) by almost entirely excluding it from his gospel; (2) by insisting at 3.3–5 that it is entirely a spiritual phenomenon, relating to a condition of a man's inner life; and (3) by affirming, here in 18.36, that this kingdom is entirely an 'other-worldly' régime which has nothing to do with earthly power and is not secured or defended by soldiers and force of arms.

In 18.36 the kingdom is referred to by Jesus as *my* Kingdom. We noticed how in both Matthew and Luke this phrase is beginning to be used as an alternative to Kingdom of God, and we interpreted it as a mark of later redactional activity rather than an authentic feature of the teaching of Jesus himself. This tendency to speak of God's Kingdom as Christ's is very understandable as Christian thinking developed. As believers came to think of Christ as invested with all the fullness of deity (e.g., Col. 2.9), the terms Christ and God became almost interchangeable words. In Paul's writings, for instance, there are several passages where one cannot be certain whether the word 'Lord' is meant to refer to Christ or to God. For Christians the moral qualities of God could be discerned by what had been revealed in Christ. He is the Truth about God. To speak of the Kingdom of God as the Kingdom of Christ helped to make it clear that the kingdom represented the values and standards by which Jesus Christ have lived and for which he died.

John makes it clear through these words ascribed to Jesus that as he understands it the Kingdom of God or of Christ has nothing to do with Jewish nationalistic aspirations or zealot activities. Some have tried to argue that Jesus had sympathies with the zealots and their guerilla tactics to achieve an independent Israel, free from foreign domination. Jesus may well have longed for the same goal, but he shows no kind of approval of the methods they were prepared to use to achieve it. His friendly attitude to both Romans and Samaritans would have alienated him sharply from these ultra-patriotic revolutionaries, as also would his teaching about loving enemies and going the second mile with them. It is, however, fairly clear that the accusation that he sympathised with nationalistic movements was an embarrassment both to Jesus himself (it was probably a contributory cause of his crucifixion) and to his followers at a later time. Mark somewhat unguardedly, perhaps unaware of the disquiet it would cause, tells how one disciple at the time of the arrest of Jesus drew a sword and cut off an ear of one of the high priest's servants (14.47). Matthew is at pains to soften this bald statement by reporting that Jesus rebuked the disciple and said: 'All who take up the sword will die by the sword' (26.52). Luke at 22.51 goes further and adds that Jesus healed the servant's ear. John does not report the incident at all, and clearly is eager to remove any suspicion that Christ's Kingdom was such as to require defending by force of arms.

We have noticed the curious fact that the phrase 'Kingdom of God', though so prevalent in the synoptics, almost disappears from the fourth gospel. In its place we find the phrase which John seems to treat as a kind of synonym for it—the phrase 'eternal life' or just 'life'. These words are found occasionally in the synoptic gospels, but in the fourth gospel they are very frequent. 'Eternal life' occurs nineteen times and 'life', bearing apparently exactly the same meaning, seventeen times. Added together this makes thirty-six instances, which is roughly similar to the number of times the Kingdom of God occurs in Matthew and Luke. John presumably preferred 'eternal life', because it emphasised those aspects of the Kingdom of God which he felt to be the essential ones, and did not include other aspects of the kingdom which he regarded as misleading.

There are one or two instances of 'eternal life' in John where the phrase has some reference to life beyond death (e.g., 5.28,29), but more often it refers quite explicitly to a quality of life available here and now (e.g., 3.36, 5.24, 6.40, 6.54); and in most other cases there can be little doubt that it this second meaning which is intended. For John, as Dodd understands it, 'the believer already enjoys eternal life'. It is, however, a quality of life wholly dependent on the person's relationship with God: it is given by God and marked by knowledge of God or fellowship with God. As such it has in it something of the dimension of eternity, the kind of life which death does not destroy. But though that aspect is not absent, the main emphasis in the phrase 'eternal life' is not on endlessness or even on life beyond death, but on a divine quality of present life which, compared with merely 'being alive', brings a new dimension of reality, authenticity or 'abundance'.

Where God establishes his rule in human life, and human life allows that rule to control and shape it, eternal life is what is created. It is this main truth about the kingdom which John wishes to emphasise. He does not wish to encourage at all the thought of the kingdom as a great divine event which takes place cosmically without the full, voluntary participation of each individual believer. Eternal life is given by God (5.26, 6.33, 10.28, 17.2) or by the Spirit of God (6.63) and is a personal experience. Man receives it only by 'believing', that is believing that God wishes to make this gift and that the believer may claim it as our own (3.15, 3.16, 3.36, 5.24, 6.47, 20.31).

Three aspects of the kingdom, therefore, are brought into special prominence by John: that it is available now, and not just at some future time; that it is wholly the gift of God; and that its coming transforms and enriches man's inner life. All three of these emphases are present also in the synoptic sayings about the kingdom, and John chooses them as the ones he wishes to underline. One may, however, doubt whether 'eternal life' may be regarded as a complete synonym for the Kingdom of God, even though it is equivalent to some aspects of it. Does the emphasis on eternal life as the gift of God tend to separate God from the gift? The Kingdom of God is God himself taking full charge of human life. In John man's part in receiving this gift is described as 'believing'. Is this quite adequate? Does not the word 'believing' omit some of the active response which the synoptic sayings insist on—e.g., the willingness to allow God to amputate elements in us which threaten to resist and thwart him? Does the phrase 'eternal life' suggest something too placid and static, rather than the small atomic bomb implied in the parables of the seed and leaven?

While we welcome the points where John brings to sharp focus certain truths about the kingdom, we may have to recognise that there are other truths to which he does less than justice.

2. NON-CANONICAL SAYINGS OF JESUS

There are a few sayings attributed to Jesus, apart from those included in the gospels, which have come down to us in the writings of the Church Fathers, the papyri discoveries at Oxyrhynchus and in the more recently found Gospel of Thomas. Of those which have reference to the Kingdom of God only two have any claim to be regarded as genuine. Origen recalls one:

He that is near me is near the fire;
He that is far from me is far from the Kingdom.

The other we owe to Tertullian; 'No man can obtain the Kingdom that has not passed through temptation'. Even if genuine it is doubtful if they add anything new to our understanding of the Kingdom of God.

3. THE ACTS OF THE APOSTLES

In the Acts of the Apostles the phrase 'the Kingdom of God' occurs much less frequently than it does in the third gospel—only seven times (Ac. 1.6 hardly qualifies to be counted as a reference to the Kingdom of *God*) as compared with thirty-one times in the gospel. Of those seven, one is a comprehensive statement that the risen Christ spoke to his disciples 'about the Kingdom of God', and another (8.12) describes Philip's preaching as concerned with 'the Kingdom of God and the name of Christ'. The remaining five instances occur in passages dealing with Paul. Whether this is due to the fact that Luke actually knew that Paul's preaching did in fact concern itself with the Kingdom of God or whether he just uses the Kingdom of as a conventional way of referring to the subject matter of the gospel, we cannot be sure.

We have already noted in Matthew and Luke the beginning of a tendency to identify Christ himself and the kingdom. Something of the same kind of thing is apparent in Acts. At 8.12 Philip's preaching is said to be concerned with the 'Kingdom of God and the name of Christ', and at 28.31 Paul, living in Rome under house arrest, is said to 'preach the Kingdom of God and teach the things concerning Jesus', an interesting combination of 'kerygma' and 'didache'. Acts cannot, however, be said to add anything to our understanding either of the original proclamation of the kingdom in the teaching of Jesus, or of its use in the later preaching of the Church.

If the Kingdom of God plays only a small part in Acts, does that mean that the truths represented by the kingdom in the teaching of Jesus have in Acts been allowed to evaporate and disappear? Has the message of God's dynamic invasion of human life, with its challenge to man to respond in total commitment and its promise of a life greatly enriched for those who do, just disappeared with the death of Jesus? Or is it rather that though the phrase itself is used less frequently, the truths it represented in the teaching of Jesus—or at least some of them—are in Acts presented under different symbols? We saw that in the fourth gospel Life or Eternal Life has in some respects replaced what was represented in the synoptics by the kingdom. Has anything similar happened in Acts?

Without doubt the truth lies in the second of these alternatives. The active power of God breaking in upon the world of men and revitalising human life, which in the synoptics is spoken of as the Kingdom of God, is here much more frequently expressed in terms of the Holy Spirit. The Spirit is the power of God ('power from on high') thrusting in upon human life and transforming it. The Holy Spirit and God's power are in constant association in the early part of Acts (e.g., 1.8, 2.4, 2.33, 5.31, 8.19, etc.). As with the kingdom so the Spirit's coming is associated with rich blessings—gladness (2.46), joy (13.52), healing (3.6), life (11.18). As with the kingdom the Spirit comes as God's gift to men (2.38,

15.8), but as a gift which needs to be received (19.2, etc.) and can indeed be declined or defied (7.51). Like the kingdom, the Spirit's activity is universal in its range (2.39; 8.25).

The Spirit in Acts is very much a present reality, and not just a future possibility. It is the fulfilment now of what God had in the past promised for some distant future (2.17,18). It is the present 'realisation' of what was once only an 'eschatological hope'. It corresponds very closely to what in the synoptic gospels is the *present* activity of the kingdom.

It is not only the great similarity between what is said in Acts about the Spirit, and what is said in the synoptic gospels about the kingdom which links them closely together. There is also the fact that, though Kingdom and Spirit appear in both the synoptic gospels and in Acts, the proportion of their appearance is approximately reversed. The kingdom predominates in the synoptics, while the Spirit is subordinate; in Acts it is the Spirit who predominates and the kingdom drops into the background. It must be that either Luke or other leaders of the Gentile mission, or both, recognised that though the kingdom had played a big part in the earliest form of the proclamation, other symbols were now more effective in conveying the same truths among Gentile hearers. For Gentile Christians the Holy Spirit better conveyed what Jesus had meant by the kingdom than a mere perpetuation of his original phrase would have done. The different audiences addressed needed to have the same truths presented in different forms. But the essential message remained the same.

6. PAUL AS AN INTERPRETER OF THE KINGDOM

When we turn to the letters of Paul we find that here too, compared with the synoptics, the Kingdom of God does not figure prominently. In all the fourteen letters ascribed to Paul in RSV (Hebrews is not included) there are only fourteen instances of its use.

Where Paul uses this phrase, it does not seem to be an expression which he freely chooses because of its current effectiveness. It sounds more like a standard term which he borrows from custom and tradition, as though he is appealing to something of recognised significance from the past. Sometimes also he introduces it as if it were a phrase which his opponents have used to support their own interpretation of the Christian life. Certainly it is remarkable how often when Paul uses the phrase it is to correct some point of view adopted by those whom he is opposing.

We shall look briefly at the various passages where Paul speaks of the Kingdom of God, and then try to co-ordinate them into a summary of what the phrase meant for Paul.

1. Rom. 14.17:

'The Kingdom of God does not mean food and drink, but righteousness, peace and joy in the Holy Spirit.

Paul is here dealing with an issue which threatens to divide the Christian community at Rome. Some Christians there have strong scruples about what a Christian should allow himself to eat. They themselves refuse to eat meat. For some of them of Jewish race this may have been because they could not buy meat which had been slaughtered by methods required by Jewish ritual laws. Their Jewish scruples continued though they had become Christians. For others it may have been that they knew that meat bought at the butchers could easily have been slaughtered as part of a sacrifice to heathen deities, and for them this made the meat unclean and defiled. Moreover those who felt these scruples had elevated them into matters of high principle which they thought every Christian ought to observe. So they accused those who differed from them of moral laxity and compromise.

Other Christians claimed that in Christ they had been set free, free from an unintelligent observance of archaic Jewish regulations, free from any superstitious notion that meat was in any way affected by being used in temple sacrifice, since the pagan gods had no existence at all except in the minds of those who believed in them. These Christians regarded themselves as the enlightened ones, and the others, with their finicking scruples, as timid, stupid and unenlightened.

Paul appeals to both groups to show consideration and respect for members of the other side, remembering that each Christian is responsible to God for his convictions, not to his fellow-Christians. Either attitude, whether of angry condemnation or sneering contempt, is totally out of place among Christians. He then tries to lift the whole argument to a higher plane, asserting that neither scruples about food nor freedom from such scruples is fundamentally important for Christian living. What matters is whether or not God rules in a person's life and this is a far wider and deeper issue than rules about diet. The evidence that God rules in a human life is found in the extent to which that life is marked by the presence of righteousness, peace and joy. The Kingdom of God means righteousness, peace and joy in the Holy Spirit.

The association of righteousness with the Kingdom of God recalls the way in which Matthew links the two (Mt. 5.10 and 20, 6.33). God's will, which is practised where God rules, is to be identified with what is right. Righteousness in the New Testament is, however, something different from mere obedience to Jewish law. Jewish righteousness put great emphasis on the fulfilment of dietary laws. Christian righteousness, however, means obedience to the will of God as revealed through Christ. Elsewhere Paul says that the perfect fulfilment of God's law is seen in 'love'; this is the perfect expression of obedience to God.

99

In a Christian community where this kind of righteousness is practised by everyone, there will be respect for one another's sincerity, forgiveness for others in their failures, a readiness to understand the difficulties another person is facing and a tolerance towards error and ignorance. In such a community there will be found peace. Right dealings and right relationships are a basic necessity if peace is to develop in any human society. So too within the human heart a consistent loyalty to what is right in personal conduct and personal relationships is the only true basis of serenity and a quiet mind.

The Kingdom of God for Paul, however, brings into being not only the quiet settled happiness of peace, but also the more radiant, jubilant happiness of joy. In the teaching of Jesus also we find that joy is associated with the Kingdom of God. In the parable of Mt. 13.44 the man who finds treasure in a field is so transported by the *joy* of his discovery that he sells all that he has to gain possession of the field, and the treasure it contains.

Righteousness, peace and joy make a splendid triad. Where God rules in human life, there they will be found, inter-related and interdependent, these three precious qualities. Then Paul adds a significant phrase: 'In the Holy Spirit'. This is not just slipped in as a concession to formal orthodoxy. For Paul the Holy Spirit signifies God's vigorous activity in human life, his invading presence. So this added phrase provides a timely reminder that 'this is all God's doing' – similar to that reminder in 2 Cor. 5.18. The Kingdom of God is not an achievement of human endeavour, nor the result of clever calculations. It becomes actual when God's Spirit takes full command in human life and is given access to every part of it, to control and inspire the whole.

We have already noted in other contexts that the Holy Spirit is often elsewhere associated with the Kingdom of God, and may even on occasions be used as a kind of equivalent of it. So in Paul one is sharply aware of the similarity between them. What Paul says here about the kingdom and what he writes about the Holy Spirit in Gal. 5.22, for instance, have much in common: 'The fruit of the Spirit is love (which for the Christian is the fulfilment of true righteousness), joy, peace, etc.'. True righteousness, peace and joy are the characteristic marks of both the Kingdom and the Holy Spirit.

This is the only reference in Romans to the Kingdom of God, but it is a very significant one. It not only gives a splendid affirmation of the moral consequences in human life when God takes charge of it, but also makes it abundantly clear that the coming of the kingdom is God's work and God's achievement. It also shows that for Paul the kingdom is a present reality in the Christian community and not just an expectation for the future.

2. I Cor. 4.20:

The Kingdom of God does not consist in talk but in power.

Curiously enough though there are only fourteen instances of 'the Kingdom of God' in the thirteen letters ascribed to Paul, no fewer than five of them occur in 1 Corinthians, far more than in any other epistle. It is also curious that the first of these (4.20) is similar in form to Rom. 14.17. It begins with a strong affirmation about what the kingdom is *not*. This suggests that some members of the church at Corinth were speaking of what 'being a Christian' meant to them in ways which were so false that Paul felt the need to deny them categorically. Moreover the whole context of the verse supports this assumption. Paul feels he must reprimand some members of the church who have been behaving 'arrogantly' (4.18). Earlier, at 4.6,7, he had rebuked them for being 'puffed up' and 'boastful'. He takes up ironically what appear to be their own haughty words with which they have described their own spiritual experiences. They had said: 'We are full to overflowing; we have become rich; we have entered our kingdom (that is, we have become kings)'. One suspects that this link between their claim to be kings and Paul's emphatic statement about the Kingdom of God is *not* accidental. It suggests that they were speaking of their entry into the Kingdom of God as a wonderful spiritual experience of ecstasy which endows them with a marked superiority over those who lacked it. It was something they could speak of with pride and self-congratulation. The writer of Revelation (1.6, 5.10) also speaks of Christians as 'kings and priests unto God'. This could be a legitimate way of humbly describing great privileges which God has bestowed. But it sounds as though some at Corinth had used such phrases as a way of elevating their own spiritual status above that of others less highly endowed. Had they really entered the Kingdom of God it would have shown itself in the way they conducted their lives rather than just in the manner in which they talked. It would have meant their humbly walking with God in complete obedience rather than congratulating themselves on their own distinctive, spiritual attainment.

So Paul firmly insists: The Kingdom of God is not a matter of talking about your own spiritual privileges, but in God-directed, effective action. God's power brings to men the ability not only to exult with him, but to suffer for him, to cope with all things, even humiliations and persecutions, through Christ who gives them strength (Phil. 4.13).

3. 1 Cor. 6.9:
Do you know that the unrighteous will not inherit the Kingdom of God.

4. 1 Cor. 6.10:
Do not be deceived: neither the immoral, nor idolaters, nor homo-sexuals, nor thieves, nor the greedy, nor drunkards, nor revilers, nor robbers will inherit the Kingdom of God.

In chapter 6 of 1 Corinthians Paul is again addressing him-self to Christians who believe themselves to be on a very high spiritual level, but behave in a very cavalier way to the ordinary decencies of life. Their watchword is: 'All things are lawful to me' (6.12). For them all that matters is their high communion with God. This has lifted them, they believe, right above mere matters of prosaic morality. Their new spiritual freedom transcends such mundane concerns. They are guilty of wronging and defrauding even their own brethren (6.8), yet they see nothing very reprehensible in it. It is an instance of the antinomianism which has undermined many religious revivals. So Paul solemnly warns them—perhaps again taking up their own boast of having found a place in God's Kingdom —that unrighteous people have no place in that kingdom. He then lists some of the types of people who are reckoned among the unrighteous. He reminds them that once, in the past, they had been like that, but that was before they were converted —'washed, sanctified and justified in the name of the Lord Jesus', 1 Cor. 6.11. All this pagan conduct should have been left behind once they made Christ King in their lives; but clearly some are becoming careless again. They have persuaded themselves somehow that such conduct is not incompatible with the Kingdom of God. To them this kingdom must have been understood as a mystical relationship with God, providing ecstatic spiritual experiences, which could be enjoyed without feeling any compelling sense of responsibility for Christ-like behaviour. Paul has to remind them that immoral conduct disqualifies people from membership in God's Kingdom.

The phrase 'inherit' the Kingdom is found also—but only very rarely—in the recorded teaching of Jesus; it must have been a phrase passed on in the tradition since it has Jewish rather than Hellenistic overtones. The word 'inherit' had probably come to mean no more than just 'gain possession of', without any sense of receiving an 'inheritance' from some deceased benefactor. It is just possible, however, that enough of its original significance had been retained for the word to suggest the 'gaining possession of something' which properly belongs to you in consequence of your membership of a family.

This inheritance is referred to as in the future: they *will* inherit. The kingdom here is future rather than present. Yet as so often with these future references, their point is not really to unveil something hidden in the future, but rather to appeal to something expected in the future as a means of emphasising what is required in the present.

It is an interesting point worth noting that when Paul here describes the present status of the Corinthians ('washed, sanctified, and justified'), which gives them hope of the future inheritance of the kingdom, he reminds them that it has all happened 'in the name of the Lord Jesus and in the Spirit of our God'. Both these phrases have been elsewhere linked with the kingdom.

5. 1 Cor. 15.23:

But each in his own order: Christ the firstfruits, then at his coming those who belong to Christ. 24. Then comes the end when he delivers the Kingdom to God the Father after destroying every rule and every authority and power.

Paul here writes in apocalyptic words about the future, describing an other-worldly transaction which lies beyond all normal historical expectations. It is a mistake to try to press for literal meanings. But as he looks into the future, Paul is able to assure believers that God's coming action to put all things right will not be chaotic and disorderly. Rather each person will have his own place in a properly arranged sequence of events.

The first to enter the transcendent kingdom will be Christ, who has been the first to rise from the dead; then those who belong to Christ, whether still living or already dead. They will enter the resurrection life 'at his coming'. And beyond that comes the end—presumably the winding up of all this earthly dispensation. Apparently at this 'end' Christ will hand over the kingdom to God the Father. The kingdom is not precisely specified as either the Kingdom of God or of Christ. But it seems as though, prior to the end, Christ is responsible for establishing this kingdom and ordering its present life, so that when the end comes he will be in a position to hand it over as a worthy achievement to God. So there is a real sense in which prior to the end the kingdom is Christ's. The kingdom seems to be Christ's in the degree that it has been realised among men. But in the final count it will be seen as God's kingdom. Before this final conclusion Christ has a vast task to accomplish, which consists of destroying 'every rule and every authority and power'. Paul appears to envisage Christ in his risen power still engaged in this developing work, which will be completed by the time of the Parousia and ready for him to hand over as a finished work to God.

Here therefore the kingdom appears to be thought of at different levels. Christ, during his earthly ministry and now in his risen power, is at work establishing and extending it. The time will come when this work is complete; then he will return to earth in glory and his coming will coincide with the end of the world order and the kingdom he has been establishing on earth will be handed over to God.

We notice, as in some of the synoptic references to God in relation to his kingdom, that the King is referred to as 'Father'.

6. 1 Cor. 15.50:

I tell you, brethren, flesh and blood cannot inherit the Kingdom of God, nor does the perishable inherit the imperishable.

This is still another instance of a Pauline saying which emphasises the type of person who will *not* be accepted into the kingdom. Here the kingdom is thought of as wholly in its future aspect—as that eternal kingdom which Christ hands over to God as the time of the End. This eternal kingdom is regarded as equivalent to what elsewhere might be called the 'resurrection life' into which Christ has already entered and which the Christian also may in due course enter through him. This resurrection life is characterised by 'power' and 'glory' (1 Cor. 15.43); it is 'imperishable' (15.42). It is also 'spiritual' in the sense that it is completely non-physical. The physical part of us will have to be left behind; only the spiritual element in us will survive. Whatever Paul meant by the resurrection of the body, he clearly did not mean that our present physical body of flesh and blood would be preserved into that resurrection life.

As elsewhere Paul is here trying to correct an error rather than merely state a truth. Probably there were those among the Christians at Corinth who spoke of their present Christian experience as a 'resurrection'. They were 'risen with Christ', a phrase Paul himself indeed used (e.g., Col. 3.1). Paul, however, insists that, no matter how deeply spiritual a Christian may be, he will still need to leave behind his body of flesh and blood and assume the new transformed 'body' which is being prepared for him.

This teaching seems to be in line with that of Jesus in Mk. 12.25 (and parallels) that in the resurrection life those who rise from the dead 'neither marry nor are given in marriage, but are like the angels of heaven'. In heaven there are no physical bodies, and so there will not be any continuation of relationship based on the needs of physical bodies.

In this passage the kingdom is equivalent to the resurrection life, or indeed to what we normally mean by 'heaven'.

7. Gal. 5.21:

The works of the flesh are plain: immorality, licentiousness, idolatry, etc. ... Those who do such things will not inherit the Kingdom of God.

As in 1 Cor. 15.50 the word 'flesh' is used to describe what will *not* be given a place in the Kingdom of God, but it is used with a different meaning. In 1 Cor. 15.50 it is used as part of the phrase 'flesh and blood' to mean merely the physical side of human life, without any suggestion that there is anything evil involved in it. In Gal. 5.21, however, it carries the other meaning, common in Paul's writings, of that in human nature which has been corrupted at its source—appetites, desires, etc.—and which, if unchecked, produces the evil things listed in verses 19 and 20. Paul, while including in it sexual immorality and drunkenness, also puts great stress on such other aspects of 'flesh' as jealousy, envy, anger, enmity, dissension, selfishness. All these things are the outward manifestation of the behaviour of human nature when it just follows its own inner impulses. In contrast, however, those 'who belong to Christ' in whom the power of the Holy Spirit is beginning to overrule natural impulses, have received from God the power which can do to death ('crucify') these evil forces, and set up opposing forces of good which will produce 'the fruit of the spirit', 'love, joy, peace, etc.' (Gal. 5.22,23).

We notice once again that this saying from Paul about the kingdom states emphatically the kind of people who will *not* gain entrance to the kingdom, as in (3), (4) and (5)—and also, implicitly in (1) and (2). It is as though he is emphatically contradicting an error which has gained currency among his readers.

There is nothing in the earlier part of Galatians to prepare the reader for a reference to the Kingdom of God. But it seems probable that there were those among the Galatian Christians who had allowed their belief in Christian freedom to run to excess, even to use it as 'an opportunity for the flesh' (Gal. 5.13), claiming that under God's forgiving grace now 'all things are permitted'. Perhaps it was in re-action against these antinomian extremists that some Christians found themselves wanting some specific guidance and authority in matters of moral conduct, such as that which the Jewish law provided. Paul has to oppose this tendency to return to the Jewish law, but here he is giving a sharp reminder to the Christians with antinomian tendencies of the requirements of the Kingdom of God. Even though the Jewish law no longer has validity for the Christian, the Rule of God in his life requires with even greater authority the total abandonment of such basically obvious evils as those named in verses 19 and 20.

8. Eph. 5.5:

No immoral man or impure man, or one who is covetous (that is, an idolater) has any inheritance in the Kingdom of Christ and of God.

Those whose concern is primarily to discover what Paul meant by the Kingdom of God will need to treat this verse with some degree of reserve, because many scholars find themselves unable to regard Ephesians as a genuinely Pauline letter in the full sense that Galatians is. It may rather be the work of a discerning disciple deriving his material as far as possible from the genuine letters of Paul.

As with much in Ephesians the verse is closely parallel to a passage in Colossians. Col. 3.5 lists the same four kinds of wickedness as Eph. 5.5, though it does not describe them as sins which prevent a man's entry into the kingdom, but rather as evil things which a Christian must not allow in his life. Similar evil things are named also in the two passages already considered from Gal. 5.21 and 1 Cor. 6.9 where the evil things which disqualify a person from entry into the kingdom are also specified.

One notices also that the kingdom is described as 'the Kingdom of Christ and of God'. Paul's earlier letters have not described the kingdom as 'Christ's', though some such thought was evidently implicit in 1 Cor. 15.24. Also in Col.

1.13 God is precisely said to have 'transferred us to the Kingdom of his beloved Son'. Already we have seen evidence that it became an increasing tendency in the early Church to speak of God's Kingdom as Christ's also.

We notice too that whereas in the other letters the idea of 'inheriting the kingdom' is referred to in the future tense, here the future reference is less explicit. The wording describes a present right rather than a future possession: '*has* no inheritance in the Kingdom'.

9. Col. 1.13:

He has delivered us from the dominion of darkness and transferred us into the kingdom of his beloved Son, in whom we have redemption, the forgiveness of sins.

Here the kingdom is described as Christ's; also it is referred to as something in the present experience of the Colossian Christians—they *hav been* already transferred into the kingdom.

This may be a case of Paul making explicit in Colossians what was implied in 1 Cor. 15.24, where the present kingdom, prior to the Parousia, is spoken of as Christ's, as he establishes it and extends it among believers; this kingdom he will hand over to God at the Parousia.

Elsewhere Paul has listed evil things which are characteristic of the environment outside God's Kingdom. Here they are referred to collectively as the 'dominion of darkness', Satan's realm.

10. Col. 4.11:

Paul's colleagues in the Christian mission are here spoken of as: 'fellow-workers for the Kingdom of God'.

This is an unusual phrase for Paul to use since it seems to imply that man's labours can serve in furthering the interest of the kingdom. Usually the kingdom represents some action by God in possessing and shaping man's life; or it is God's reign in which a man may enter or gain a place. Here Christians can co-operate in the aims of the Kingdom and by what they do to further its interests. This idea has proved very attractive to twentieth-century Christians, who have welcomed any emphasis on man's part in the achievement, but it is not typical of Paul.

11. 1 Thess. 2.12:
We exhorted you ... to lead a life worthy of God, who calls you into his own Kingdom and glory.

The phrase 'to call you into' reminds us of the synoptic way of talking of man 'entering' the kingdom. It is not clear whether Paul thinks of the kingdom here as something in the future which men look forward to and seek to make themselves fit for, or whether it is a present privilege they may enter into now. The presence of the word 'glory' may perhaps incline us to think that it refers to the future, but Paul can use 'glory' of present privileges as well as future ones, as when he speaks of the 'glorious freedom of the children of God'. Glory may be said to be applicable to any set of circumstances where God is given his rightful place.

At any rate, 'to lead a life worthy of God' is a proper response to God's summons to enter his kingdom.

12. 2 Thess. 1.5:
The fact that the Thessalonian Christians are proving themselves steadfast under persecution enables Paul to write:
This is evidence of the righteous judgement of God that you may be made worthy of the Kingdom of God for which you are suffering.

It is interesting, but perhaps only a coincidence, that the word 'worthy' occurs in both the passages from the Thessalonian letters in which the kingdom is mentioned. But in each case the emphasis is on the clear obligation of those who accept the Kingdom of God into their lives to allow God really to rule in their lives and shape their conduct.

Perhaps it is best to regard the kingdom in both these instances as neither wholly present or wholly future, but rather as a relationship with God available to Christians, which has one dimension in the present and another in the ultimate future. So for Paul justification in the present is wholly of grace, but in the final judgement man's response to the great privilege of freely offered justification will count greatly in the final verdict. The present kingdom is God's free gift to man in his unworthiness. The future kingdom is for those whose response to that free gift has been 'worthy'.

13. 2 Tim. 4.1:

I charge you in the presence of God and of Christ ... and by his appearing and his Kingdom.

Most scholars seem to agree that in their present form the pastoral epistles cannot be regarded as actually letters from Paul, though many think they include genuinely Pauline material. In this particular passage the degree of uncertainty is increased because it is not clear here how the Greek words ought to be translated. But it is apparent that here the kingdom is associated with the Parousia. The writer bases his appeal to his readers on two truths which both they and he confidently accept—the certainty of the future coming of Christ in glory and of his rule (his Kingdom) which will from that time be firmly established.

14. 2 Tim. 4.18:

The Lord will rescue me from every evil and save me for his heavenly Kingdom.

The apostle writes that God has rescued him in the past from evil things which have threatened to engulf him, and he is, therefore, confident that God will continue to save him in the future hazards that life may bring, and finally place him in the heavenly kingdom. Here the thought is of a future kingdom, a kingdom 'in heaven'.

In reviewing these various references to the Kingdom of God in Paul's writings one gains the impression that none of them represents a freely-chosen, spontaneous manner of speech. Paul appears to use the phrase with a certain formality. He seems either to appeal to it as a phrase hallowed by tradition whose authority all Christians accept, or refer to it as a phrase which has been inaccurately interpreted by his opponents, against whose usage he must protest and whose error he must try to correct.

The features of the kingdom which Paul emphasises may be analysed as follows:

(a). One remarkable feature of this relatively small group of sayings is that two of them are taken up with negative statements, stressing what the Kingdom of God is NOT. In I Cor. 4.20 Paul says emphatically that the Kingdom of God is *not* a matter of 'talk' but of 'action'; and in Rom. 14.17 he insists with equal urgency that it does *not* consist in observing prescribed rules of diet, but rather in such universally valued qualities as righteousness, peace and joy.

(b). The second prominent feature of these sayings is the extreme emphasis Paul places on the moral content of the kingdom. In I Cor. 6.9 Paul insists that wicked people will not inherit the kingdom and proceeds to enumerate the kinds of wickedness which excludes them. Similar affirmations and lists are found also in Gal. 5.21 and Eph. 5.5. The kinds of wickedness which for Paul excludes people from the kingdom reveal something of his understanding of the nature of the kingdom. In I Cor. 6.10 ten forms of wickedness are named; five are sexual and one other is drunkenness. So the emphasis here is largely on the undisciplined satisfactions of physical appetites and desires. The other four condemned sins are robbery, dishonesty, covetousness and reviling. In Gal. 5.19 the list is longer, containing fifteen kinds of wickedness. Of these only three are sexual; also included are the use of magic, drunkenness and idolatry; but no fewer than eight describe attitudes which are mainly of the kind which cause the disruption of happy and harmonious relationships in a community, such things as strife, enmity, jealousy, envy, anger, dissension, etc.

In these contexts the thought of the kingdom is future, but the purpose of referring to it is not to tell the readers something they did not know about the hidden things still to come, but to use the thought of that future kingdom as a sanction for enforcing here and now in this present life conduct appropriate to the hope of that future privilege.

Two others of the sayings also have the effect of emphasising the importance of present conduct, by insisting that Christians must allow in themselves only conduct which is worthy of the kingdom (1 Thess. 2.12, 2 Thess. 1.5). The moral character of the kingdom is therefore of supreme importance to Paul.

A corollary of this firm exclusion of different kinds of evil from the kingdom is the claim that within the kingdom are to be found only the highest standards in matters of self-control, both in regard to sexual conduct and other appetites. Honesty, restrained speech and concern for others are marks of life within the kingdom. Also characteristic of the kingdom are those qualities in people which make for stable community life—goodwill, humility, meekness, loyalty and mutual appreciation. It is not so much that these qualities are required as a pre-condition for entering the kingdom; rather they are the marks of those who have been brought under the effective control of God's spirit. To claim to be in the kingdom but to deny God the right to rule your life is to merit Christ's rebuke to those who say 'Lord, Lord' but to fail to do what the Lord commands.

To sum it up, we may therefore say that 'righteousness' for Paul is an essential component of the kingdom, as indeed he writes quite explicitly at Rom. 14.17. For Paul righteousness is mainly the work of God. It is God putting wrong things right. It is an active not a static element in the life of God, far more than just a standard of good behaviour. It can also be used to describe what we call 'a right relationship with God', the privilege that the Christian may come to enjoy of knowing that his own evil and alienated life has been accepted by God—and this too is God's doing. Righteousness also is that conduct which results from this right relationship of obedience to God; it is a pattern of upright conduct in personal matters, of conduct which also fully respects the rights and feelings of others, and makes concern for their welfare a guiding principle of life. All these elements within 'righteousness' are gathered up in Paul's use of the phrase 'The Kingdom of God'.

(c). We saw earlier in the sayings of Jesus that the Kingdom of God sometimes referred to something actively present in his own ministry. At other times it referred to a future dimension. The same is true of Paul's uses. Sometimes it means something here and now, sometimes it is something in the future; sometimes both dimensions seem to be present in the same saying.

(i). Those with predominantly a future emphasis include the instances where a verb in the future tense is used, as, for example, 'will inherit the kingdom', in (3), (4), (6), (7), though we have already noticed that even in these references the main purpose of the appeal to the future kingdom is to enforce the importance of certain kinds of conduct in the present.

Some features of that future kingdom are, however, revealed. In 1 Cor. 15.50 (6) the future kingdom is declared to be entirely a community of spiritual beings, in which our present physical bodies cannot conceivably have any part. Also in 1 Cor. 15.23 (5) we noted that the present dimension of the kingdom is represented as under the direction of Christ, who after the Parousia and the end of the world will hand it over in its completed form to God himself.

The two references in the Pastoral epistles, (13) and (14), are both predominantly future. (13) precisely associates the Kingdom with the Parousia, and (14) links it with a verb in the future tense.

(ii). There are, however, other statements in Paul about the kingdom which emphasise its present significance. In Col. 1.13 an unmistakably past tense of the verb is used: 'God rescued us from darkness and transferred us into the Kingdom of his beloved Son'. It can, however, be argued that the Kingdom of Christ the Son is not wholly identical with the Kingdom of God, that it is only an anticipatory foretaste of the Kingdom of God which is still to come. And this contention is supported by 1 Cor. 15.24 where the kingdom as men know it here is what Christ is achieving on earth, and this he will in due course hand over to God. But the present Kingdom of Christ is best understood as one aspect of the Kingdom of God rather than something wholly different.

Eph. 5.5 also uses a present tense, not a future one. No deliberately wicked person *has* any inheritance in the Kingdom of God. The phrasing here is not distinctively present or future. An inheritance may be regarded as something which belongs to the heir now, because of the owner's promise about the future, but the actual possession of it as his own does not come till later.

There are, however, two other passages where the present reference is clear beyond any ambiguity. In Rom. 14.17 Paul insists that the Kingdom of God is not concerned with pre-scribing what a person may or may not eat and drink. Its con-cerns are with righteousness, peace and joy in the Holy Spirit. Righteousness, peace and joy should therefore be the present concerns of the Roman Christians, because these qualities are the mark of God's Kingdom. Moreover the introduction of the Holy Spirit anchors the thought in the present. The Holy Spirit represents God's active power at work in this world, not in some future life. Indeed for Paul the gift of the Holy Spirit is the foretaste (*arrabon*) now of the life of heaven still to come (2 Cor. 5.5). The Holy Spirit is the mark of God's Kingdom in its present operation.

This use of the kingdom with sometimes a present and sometimes a future reference is not careless inconsistency on Paul's part. It is characteristic of Paul's whole view of the Christian life. For him God's gifts had *already* been received through Christ—in a preliminary but very real measure; but what had already been received was but a foretaste; it was not yet the full measure; that was still to come. Redemption, for instance, is spoken of as both present and future. (Rom. 3.24, cf. Rom. 8.23). So also is adoption (Rom. 8.15, cf. Rom. 8.23).

So it is with the Kingdom of God. Men can live in it now, draw on its strength and vitality and guidance, and embody its qualities in their own manner of living. In this anticipatory stage it is all so clearly the work of Christ in human lives that it is natural for the Christian to think of it as something that can be called Christ's Kingdom without its being thought of as really different from the Kingdom of God. The kingdom on earth is, however, not the conclusion of the matter. Though the kingdom has a base of operations amid human life on earth, the fulness of its life lies beyond this earthly sphere, in heaven or in eternity, in the completion of God's purposes which do not reach their end within the limits of human life on earth.

(d). Paul writes his letters to Christians who, he believes, have already accepted God's Kingdom into their lives, or, to put the same truth in different words, have gained a place within God's Kingdom. Because of this they expect to be assured of a place in the completed kingdom, when, at some future time, it is finally established after the Parousia. In his letters, therefore, because they are addressed to mature Christians he does not attempt to provide elementary teaching about the way to gain entrance to the kingdom. His main concern is that his readers, already Christians living within God's Kingdom, should live worthily of it, and that they should put into practice the life of the kingdom now so as to ensure that they retain their place in it and do not find themselves excluded from its glorious future.

(e). Although Paul does not make the kingdom the main vehicle of his message as Jesus appears to have done, his references to the kingdom do, however, have much in common with the synoptic picture. Righteousness, for instance, is an essential part of it, as it was for Matthew, cf. Rom. 14.17 (1). Similarly the kingdom raises the quality of a man's inward life (its 'blessedness'), bringing him peace and joy, and even 'glory' (1) and (11). It also brings with it salvation (14). Its coming and its power is the work of the Holy Spirit of God, and therefore something God himself achieves (1). The tendency to speak of God's Kingdom as in certain respects Christ's is also present in Paul as well as in the synoptics (5), (9), (13), (14). Even though in relation to the kingdom it would be more appropriate to speak of God as King, both Paul and the synoptics introduce the word 'Father' (5) and (9). There is therefore no substantial difference between Paul's use and that of Jesus.

Compared with the synoptics, however, the Kingdom of God appears only occasionally in Paul. Does this mean that in Paul some of the truths about the kingdom in the proclamation of Jesus have been reduced in significance or unduly neglected? Or is it that Paul finds other ways of expressing these truths? It is undoubtedly the second of these options.

Much of the message embodied in the words of Jesus: 'The

Kingdom of God is at hand' is represented in Paul by his use of the Holy Spirit. What the synoptics say about the Kingdom of God and what Paul writes about the Holy Spirit are strikingly parallel. Both are the bringers of righteousness, both come to man as God's gift, both bring to human experience rich privileges, such as salvation, peace, joy, life. Both require a response on the part of the believer and do not totally override his responsible decision. Both come into human life with an accession of power. For Paul, working in the context of the Gentile mission, the message proclaimed in terms of the Spirit held certain advantages over the Kingdom phraseology, or at least was free from some disadvantages. But the message, whether proclaimed in one way or the other, was substantially the same.

7. THE OTHER NEW TESTAMENT WRITERS

There are two references to God's Kingdom in Hebrews. The first is at 1.8: 'The righteous sceptre is the sceptre of thy Kingdom' (a quotation from Ps. 45.6,7). Two points here are worth noting: 'righteousness' is accepted as an integral part of the Kingdom of God; and the words of the psalm, originally addressed to God, are here interpreted as spoken 'of the Son'. The kingdom is Christ's Kingdom.

The second reference is at 12.28 where the readers are exhorted: 'Therefore let us be grateful for receiving a Kingdom that cannot be shaken'. The word 'receive' is one that recurs in the synoptic tradition in sayings about the kingdom. It implies that the kingdom is God's gift to those who will accept it. The context does not indicate unmistakably whether the kingdom is here thought of as present or still to come, but the word 'receiving' (which is a continuous present tense in the Greek and means, 'since we are receiving') suggests something already present in the experience of the readers, rather than something wholly future. The whole context also suggests that the cause of their gratitude is that amid all that is transient in the world of time and sense they nevertheless possess in the kingdom something that does not fail and pass away. The probability, therefore, is that the writer thinks of the kingdom as a present spiritual treasure which in the future cannot be destroyed by the disasters which are to overwhelm all material things. This present reality of the kingdom is confirmed in Heb. 6.5 where the writer, though he does not actually use the word 'kingdom' does nevertheless affirm with the utmost certainty the reality of the *present* privileges of Christian believers. Theirs is not merely a hope of future good, but an enjoyment of much that is good in the immediate present: they 'have been enlightened; they have tasted the heavenly gift; they have become partakers of the Holy Spirit; they have tasted the goodness of the word of God and the powers of the age to come'. What are called the 'powers of the world to come' are already sufficiently present for the readers to have tasted them. This suggests that the kingdom is thought of as a present anticipation of a larger fulfilment in the future.

This kingdom 'cannot be shaken': it is an 'everlasting' kingdom, a kingdom which will endure for ever and ever.

There is only one reference to the kingdom in James: 'Has not God chosen those who are poor in the world to be rich in faith and heirs of the Kingdom which he has promised to those who love him' (2.5).

The kingdom appears here to be thought of as mainly, if not entirely, in the future, since it is spoken of as 'promised'. One could argue, however, that the promise was made in the past and that possession of the kingdom in the present is spoken of as a fulfilment of that past promise. We notice in this reference echoes of other features of the kingdom which have already been noted elsewhere: (1). It is God's gift to man, not man's achievement. God has *chosen* those who are to be recipients of it. (2). It is associated with the 'poor' as in the first beatitude, and reminds us of the words of Jesus about the difficulty of the rich gaining entry to the kingdom. (3). The use of the word 'heir' recalls the recurring phrase about 'inheriting the kingdom'. (4). There is a response required from those to whom the kingdom is offered. Here the response is that of 'loving God', which in Luke's gospel is the response appropriate to those who are overwhelmed with gratitude for the forgiveness they have received from God (Lk. 7.47–48).

The one reference in 2 Peter (1.11) is to the future dimension of the kingdom: 'So there will be richly provided for you an entrance into the eternal Kingdom of our Lord and Saviour Jesus Christ'. Entrance into the kingdom *will be provided* in the future; it is here only a promise and a hope. We note the traditional thought of man 'entering' the kingdom, and also the fact that the kingdom is described, not as God's, but as that 'of our Lord and Saviour Jesus Christ'. The adjective 'eternal' recalls the thought of an 'everlasting

Kingdom' and of a kingdom which cannot be shaken (Heb. 12.28).

A quick glance at a concordance gives the impression that the kingdom is fairly prominent in the book of the Revelation. The word occurs nine times; but in fact only five of these refer to God's Kingdom. One would expect that in a book which is so notoriously apocalyptic in its outlook these references to the kingdom would be unquestionably in the future tense. But this is not so.

(a) Rev. 1.6:

He made us a Kingdom, priests to his God and Father ...

This passage describes the privileges which Christ 'the first born of the dead and the ruler of kings on earth' has already bestowed on his followers: 'He loves us and has freed us from our sins by his blood and made us a kingdom, priests to his God and Father'. 'He has made us a Kingdom'. The initiative, as always, is from God's side, not man's, but here it is Christ rather than God who has taken the action. God, however, is closely related to this action, since it has been done for him: it is *for God* through Christ's action that believers have become a kingdom and priests. The curious characteristic we have noted elsewhere also appears here: even in the context of the kingdom God is spoken of as Father.

It is unexpected to find Christian people described as the 'kingdom'. Some of the older translations introduced an interpretative element and took the liberty of translating the word 'kingdom' as 'kings', to make it parallel with 'priests'. It may even be that this is what the writer had in mind, though he did in fact use the word 'kingdom'. N.E.B. translates it as 'royal house'. Christ, acting for God, has raised Christians to the status of members of the King's household, the royal family. The kingdom is the family of the King, and Christians are within that family. Perhaps the meaning is not much different from Paul's affirmation that Christians have been given 'sonship' ('adoption') within God's family, the family of their Father, though the writer of Revelation couches it all in more impressive words. It may have been this somewhat high-sounding phraseology that sometimes encouraged the more pretentious among Christians to make the kind of extravagant claims which Paul has to rebuke in 1 Cor. 4.8: 'You have become kings'.

(b) Rev. 1.9:

I John, your brother, who share with you in Jesus the tribulation and the Kingdom and the patient endurance ...

It is peculiar to find the kingdom sandwiched in between tribulation and patient endurance, as though in the writer's thought it belongs within the same range of ideas. One would assume that its main emphasis here is, therefore, on the Rule of God which from the point of view of the Christian believer means 'obedience' to the will of God. Its emphasis is not on the privilege of the kingdom, but on the cost involved in maintaining that privilege. The kingdom is clearly a present factor in the experience of the Christians, not something in the future only. It is not clearly indicated whether the kingdom is thought of primarily as God's or Christ's, but it is the Christians' relation to Jesus which involves them in the kingdom.

(c) Rev. 5.10:

Thou hast made them a Kingdom and priests to God, and they shall reign on the earth.

This is part of a song addressed to 'the Lamb'. The words bear some, though not a close, resemblance to Is. 61.6. Kingdom and priests are here associated, as earlier in 1.6, as if they were parallel expressions, and it is the Christians who are described as the kingdom. The one who has given them this status is Christ himself. It is a present gift, not just a promise for the future. But there is also contained within it a hope for the future: 'they shall reign'. Oddly, it is the Christians who are to reign, not God or Christ.

(d) Rev. 11.15:

The kingdom of the world has become the Kingdom of our Lord and of his Christ, and he will reign for ever and ever.

These words are proclaimed by 'loud voices in heaven'. Once again the kingdom is something which has already been achieved, though some might argue that this wording is a device for proclaiming the utter certainty of what is planned in the near future, something which is so sure to happen that the writer can speak of it as already an accomplished fact. God and Christ, it is proclaimed, have become effective rulers in the world where previously their rivals held sway. The kingdom is acclaimed as both God's and Christ's, though Christ is clearly in a subordinate role as God's servant, since he is described as 'God's Christ'. It is not clear whether the writer means God or Christ as the one who will reign for ever.

(e) Rev. 12.10:

Now the salvation and the power and the Kingdom of God and the authority of his Christ have come ...

This is the only passage in Revelation where the full phrase 'the Kingdom of God' is used. Here as elsewhere it is associated with God's power and God's salvation. Associated with the kingdom is the idea of God's effective intervention (power) for the restoration of human life (salvation). Once again it is in close association with Christ, and Christ, as in 11.15, is described as 'God's Christ'—God's appointed servant doing the will of God. One wonders if the writer felt there was any distinction between the Kingdom of God and what he calls 'the authority of his Christ'. The kingdom 'has come'; it has already happened, but, as before, this could be understood as an emphatic way of representing the nearness and certainty of something soon about to happen.

In Revelation, therefore, we find that many truths already found in sayings about the kingdom in other books of the New Testament re-appear. The kingdom has both present and future dimensions; it comes by God's initiative and action, an initiative which may be carried into effect by Christ. We find that related to the kingdom is the thought of God as Father, and of his power to achieve salvation for men. What, however, is peculiar to this book is the curious way of speaking of Christian believers as themselves 'the kingdom'. Since, however, in this sense 'the kingdom' is used as a parallel to the word 'priests' (not priesthood), and since the writer's use of Greek is somewhat erratic and unusual, one cannot be quite sure what meaning he meant 'the kingdom' to carry in these two contexts (1.6 and 5.10). It would be unwise to try to draw any firm conclusion from these passages. It is, however, unusual to find those who have been received into the kingdom spoken of as though they are to be identified with it.

8. AN ASSESSMENT OF THE INTERPRETERS OF THE KINGDOM

The theme of the Kingdom of God was central in the teaching of Jesus. The synoptic gospels make this quite clear. In the other books of the New Testament, however, the phrase occurs much less frequently, so that one gains the impression that in the generation after Jesus the phrase became one venerated in the tradition rather than one which speakers and writers spontaneously chose as a vivid and meaningful vehicle of their message for their own time. Sometimes, however, it seems as though extreme elements on the fringe of the Church may have used it for their own unbalanced teaching, so that when Paul, for instance, mentions it, it is with the purpose of correcting the misuse.

The writers who do use the phrase reflect in the main the meaning Jesus gave to it, though we do find that sometimes new elements are introduced or elements already there are picked out for special emphasis. At the same time, as references to the kingdom become less frequent, we find that the same spiritual truths which Jesus affirmed by means of the Kingdom of God are proclaimed by these other writers under different symbols. It is not that the message of the kingdom is diminished; rather it is expressed in other words.

How far do these variations successfully re-affirm the message of Jesus himself about the kingdom? Or to what extent do they distort it? We look first at the way they used the expression 'Kingdom of God' and the meaning they gave to it, and then at the alternative ways they adopted to proclaim the same truths.

We noted that in Matthew the phrase 'the Kingdom of God' is almost entirely replaced by its synonym 'the Kingdom of Heaven'. It cannot be said with certainty which phrase Jesus himself used, though most scholars would opt for 'the

Kingdom of God'. What is certain is that in the New Testament no writer other than Matthew adopted Matthew's phrase. In all other books of the New Testament it is spoken of as the Kingdom of God.

Secondly, the fact that in the coming of the kingdom it is God who is taking the initiative is never lost sight of. The kingdom is never just a moral state of affairs which man by his own good conduct and hard endeavours can hope to establish —as some modern writers have understood it. Man's part consists in his response to what God has done or is doing or offering. Man's response, however, is nevertheless an essential element. The kingdom is never seen as a process of remorseless and inevitable fate to which man can only submit. Nor is it God acting in such a way as to sweep aside man's hesitation or opposition as unimportant and irrelevant. What God is doing invites man's accepting response, and indeed exerts pressure on man to respond obediently; but man's response may in the end be nothing but refusal and rejection.

Also, if we take the interpreters as a whole, they recognise that in the kingdom there are both present and future aspects. Without doubt the kingdom is to some degree already at work in the world of men and indeed has already won certain achievements. But the complete coming is not yet. What has already happened is only a small beginning—a kind of foretaste—of a much greater fulfilment which lies ahead in the future. Usually this fulfilment can be thought of as a spiritual mode of life beyond death, corresponding to what is commonly meant by 'heaven'. Sometimes it is seen as a great advancement of God's rule here in the world of men. Sometimes it is combined with apocalyptic hopes and associated with coming events of a spectacular and cosmic nature which will bring the normal course of history to its end.

Another basic truth which is everywhere recognised is that the kingdom, whether here on earth in its present realisation or in its future fulness, is rich in blessings for those who have accepted it and identified themselves with it. The kind of words used by the interpreters to express these blessings are 'peace', 'joy', 'life', and 'salvation' (an all-embracing word which includes all the others).

Similarly, as in the teaching of Jesus, we find that the kingdom is spoken of as a 'gift' from God, to be 'received' or 'entered' or 'inherited'. The word 'power' is also associated with its coming. Moreover the King who rules in the kingdom and extends its boundaries and overcomes its enemies is still —oddly enough—spoken of as Father, as though the relationships within God's Kingdom are most like those within a well-ordered family.

Among the interpreters of the Kingdom of God we do, however, find certain differences from the teaching of Jesus. Some of these are not really more than a heightened and more explicit emphasis on elements in the Kingdom of God which in his teaching were implied or assumed rather than explicitly insisted on. Others are deliberate additions. Among these 'innovations' in the interpreters, there are four which can be welcomed, because they not only proved valuable in conveying the message of the kingdom to the Christians of their own time, but also for modern preachers they provide the means of drawing the attention of their hearers to real aspects in the message of the kingdom.

There is, however, one of these 'innovations' which several of the interpreters include, indicating that it had become widespread in the belief of the early Church, which in our judgement misrepresents the original teaching of Jesus, and also proves to be an embarrassment to the modern Christian. This is the identification of the coming of the kingdom with an apocalyptic event expected within a few years at most. It is clear from the New Testament that many in the early Church came to believe that Christ himself would soon return to the world in triumph and glory. His earthly ministry had ended with an ignominious death on a Roman cross, but within three days that defeat had been transformed into victory by his resurrection from the dead. This success, however, was understood to be only a foretaste of the final victory which would be his when he came again to this earth. This second coming would be one of universal triumph when all his enemies would be subdued. We read about this confident expectation in Paul's two letters to the Thessalonians (especially 1 Thess. 4.14–18 and 2 Thess. 2.1–8), and also, in somewhat less exuberant words, in 1 Cor. 15.23–28.

Some interpreters of the kingdom identified the coming of the kingdom, for which Jesus had taught men to pray, with this expected coming of Christ, who is often spoken of in this connection as 'Son of Man'. Matthew and Luke both seem to have done this and in places have re-phrased sayings of Jesus about the kingdom to associate its coming with the Parousia. Matthew, for instance, in 16.28, adapts Mk. 9.1 in order to achieve this identification, and so too Luke at 21.31 changes the wording of Mk. 13.29 to achieve the same end. But this seems to be clearly the work of the two evangelists rather than an accurate recording of what Jesus himself had said.

This association of the coming of the kingdom and the Parousia became common in the early Church. Paul seems to imply it in 1 Cor. 15.24 when he speaks of Christ delivering the kingdom to God in the final days. Also at 2 Tim. 4.1 'his appearing and his Kingdom' are brought together in a single phrase. On the whole, however, it was the Parousia which was the focus of attention and only occasionally do we find the coming of the kingdom identified with it. Elsewhere when the kingdom is spoken of in its future aspect the reference may often be more naturally understood as directed either to some great spiritual advance on earth or else to 'heaven', the spiritual realm beyond this earth where God rules supreme and where his servants serve him and delight in his company.

This Parousia of Christ was clearly an intense reality in the expectation of first century Christians. The coming of the kingdom would in the fulfilment of God's purposes coincide with the coming of Christ and all this would happen within the lifetime of some who heard Jesus speak the words. So too when Paul wrote to the Thessalonians he had no doubt that the Parousia would take place within the lifetime of most of those to whom he wrote. Indeed the awkward problem was to be sure that those who happened to die before the event would not be deprived of their full share in it. But neither Matthew's nor Paul's expectation was in fact fulfilled. All contemporaries of Jesus and all first generation Christians in Thessalonia died and the Parousia had not happened. Since then more than sixty generations have gone by. Only a few in each generation still manage to reinterpret the biblical evidence to make it apply to their own time. Nor do people of our time find it easy to imagine how such a coming would take place today. Only those who take a strictly literalist view of scripture give any real place to it in their faith, and in so doing they lay on their shoulders the intolerable burden (for literalists) of trying to explain why what had clearly been promised in scripture within a generation or so of the death of Jesus did not in fact take place.

As we have noted earlier, during the last fifty years or so there has developed a kind of scholarly orthodoxy which has asserted, usually without providing any strong evidence to prove it, that it was Jesus himself who identified the coming of the kingdom with his own Parousia. We have seen reason to doubt this—quite apart from the more general doubt whether Jesus himself would indeed have been in error on a matter of such importance. The sayings ascribed to Jesus which make this identification do not belong to the earliest form of the tradition, but bear the marks of editorial redaction. In consequence of the actual evidence there is now a new mood of independence arising among scholars which takes leave to challenge the former orthodoxy, and claim that the Parousia sayings in the gospels do not belong to the teaching of Jesus himself but to the post-resurrection Church.

It was, therefore, characteristic of some early interpreters of the kingdom in New Testament times to identify the coming of the kingdom with the Parousia, and to insinuate words expressing this opinion into some of the sayings of Jesus. The identification was not, however, derived from that teaching in the first place, nor is it a form of presenting the kingdom which offers help to a modern exponent. It may have been of value to the early Christian, and some Christians of later times have tried to revive it as a means of rousing new hopes and expectations. But on the whole we do not believe that it offers any real help today to those who wish to understand what the kingdom meant for Jesus or to apply its meaning to the life and times of modern Christians.

The adaptions which the interpreters have introduced into

their representation of the Kingdom of God are not all distortions of the teaching of Jesus. Four of them at least may be said to bring out prominently elements which were already there, and at the same time to provide modern exponents with useful words and phrases for interpreting what the kingdom means for people of today. These four consist of the association of the Kingdom of God with the following concepts: (1) Righteousness; (2) Life; (3) The Holy Spirit; and (4) Christ himself.

1. Righteousness

The word 'righteousness' seems to be so firmly embedded in our thought of the teaching of Jesus, and indeed in his teaching about the kingdom, that it comes at first as a surprise to find that of the four evangelists Matthew is the only one who attributes the use of this word to Jesus. It is true that the corresponding adjective 'righteous' is found more frequently on the lips of Jesus, but even this word usually carries an ironical quality as though Jesus used it mainly, not of the genuinely righteous but of the 'so-called' or 'self-styled' righteous. Instances of its use are: 'I did not come to call the righteous (Mk. 2.17), and 'There is more joy in heaven over one repentant sinner than over ninety-nine righteous people' (Lk. 15.7).

This suggests that the words 'righteous' and 'righteousness' had for Jesus become slightly tainted words, because of the meaning they had come to carry in common usage. Among the Pharisees and their adherents these words were used of deeply religious people who kept with scrupulous exactness all the legal and ritual observances required by the Mosaic law, with its concentration on outward actions like sabbath-keeping, fixed times for praying, and regulated fasting and almsgiving. Certainly when Matthew represents Jesus as teaching that one's 'righteousness' ought not to be advertised for all to see but rather be the private expression of man's devotion to God the modes of 'righteousness' he specifically named were fasting, praying and almsgiving. This restriction in current usage of the great Old Testament word 'righteousness' to mean ritual observances (rather than justice and mercy and consideration for others) may well account for the unexpected manner in which Jesus seems to have avoided the word. Had Jesus used it in its true prophetic sense his hearers might well have misunderstood it to mean only the trivial routines to which they themselves had reduced it.

Yet there is no doubt that in the true sense of what is 'right', as the Old Testament prophets understood and used the word, the Kingdom of God is greatly concerned with it. It seems likely that to express this deeper sense of the word Jesus preferred to use the phrase 'the will of God' or 'the will of my Father'. Though the Pharisees no doubt believed that what they understood as 'righteousness' was also the will of God, the real will of God was much less formalised and codified and rigid. As such it was a concept which Jesus himself could more easily invest with the meaning he wished to give it.

The basic idea behind the term 'Kingdom of God' was felt to be so obvious that the evangelists seem to have felt no need to emphasise it. It means the humble acknowledgement of God as supreme ruler by all who think of themselves as within his kingdom. Those who receive the kingdom, or enter it, are those who obey God as subjects obey their king, those for whom the will of God is supreme, of far greater authority than their own desires, or the demands and threats of other human beings (cf. Acts 5.29). This total obedience to God is of a kind that may involve the loss of what most people value most highly in their own lives—hand, foot, eye. It may mean the abandonment of treasured privileges such as wealth, and the subordination of life's dearest relationships—parents, wife, children. In personal matters it will mean loving neighbours no less than self, doing for others what we should like others to do for us, even loving enemies in the sense of honestly seeking their good rather than acting out of revenge. It means a readiness to forgive injuries, and to discard resentment. This is the new righteousness; this is the 'law and the prophets' in the form in which Jesus had brought it to fulfilment. If he personally had avoided the use of the word 'righteousness' because in his time it would have been open to serious misunderstanding, the later followers of Jesus found themselves able to use it again because for them it had been refurnished with its true meaning through all that Jesus taught and all that he himself had been.

So it was that Matthew, for whom 'righteousness' now meant the will of god as interpreted by Jesus, felt that he could confidently use it to explain to a later generation what the Kingdom of God meant. Jesus, according to Luke 12.31 had said: 'Seek the Kingdom of God' (instead of being preoccupied with anxiety about food and clothes). Matthew, reproducing the same unit of teaching, at the same time elaborates it a little so as to bring the meaning out more clearly, and writes: 'Seek first the Kingdom of God *and his righteousness* . . .' With a similar intention, where in Luke Jesus teaches men to pray: 'Your Kingdom come', Matthew tried to give a practical application to the prayer by an addition: 'Your Kingdom come; *your will be done*, on earth as in heaven'.

Paul, no less than Matthew, is well aware that in its true sense of obedience to the will of God in matters of conduct 'righteousness' is very much an integral part of the kingdom. It is not only that he insists again and again that persistently immoral people have no place in the God's Kingdom (1 Cor. 6.9,10; Gal. 5.21, etc.), but in Rom. 14.17 he affirms: 'The Kingdom of God *is* righteousness' (as well as peace and joy). Heb. 1.8 carries the same implication.

It is not that a person has to make himself righteous before he can enter or receive the kingdom. Rather it is that as he does receive the kingdom into his life, he puts his life under the sovereign command of God so that God's saving power begins to cleanse and order it. The rule of God in human life extends and deepens its hold till evil is increasingly excluded and replaced by good, and wrong relationships with other people are replaced by a loving concern for their welfare. Some people, as we saw, were so opposed to the 'moralisation' of the Christian faith that they could speak of the Kingdom of God entirely in terms of inward experience and spiritual ecstasy and illumination, so that by comparison 'mere morality' represented only a 'lower level' of religion that a truly spiritual person was able to transcend. But though it is true that the kingdom does bring joy and peace and illumination, it also brings 'righteousness'; and where deliberate wickedness persists and is treated casually as of no significance for the 'spiritually advanced' Christian, that can only mean in fact that there the kingdom has not come, God's will is not being obeyed, and those who claim that it has are only imagining it.

Paul insists that love is the true fulfilment of the Law. For the Jew the fulfilment of the Law was righteousness. So Paul could equally have said that love (in the sense of an honest, practical concern for the welfare of others) is the fulfilment of righteousness. The new righteousness of Jesus, the truly Christian righteousness, is love for others. Paul who wrote that the Kingdom of God is righteousness, peace and joy might equally have written that the Kingdom of God is *love*, peace and joy, as elsewhere he did indeed write that love, joy, peace were the 'fruit of the Spirit'.

2. Life

'Life' or 'eternal life' almost entirely replaces the phrase 'the Kingdom of God' in the Fourth Gospel. 'Kingdom of God' occurs in it only twice but life appears no fewer than forty-six times. Clearly that aspect of the Kingdom of God which may be described as 'life' is the one which this evangelist believed to be of most importance.

This use of 'life' in John as a kind of equivalent for the kingdom is not an entirely new innovation, though the degree in which he uses it is exceptional. There are instances of it also in the synoptics. It occurs, for instance, in that stern saying of Jesus about the possible need to sacrifice hand, foot or eye, if God's greatest blessings are to be gained. In two instances that blessing is called 'life'; in the third instance it is changed to 'the Kingdom of God' (Mk. 9.43ff.). Similarly when the young man asks: 'What am I to do to gain eternal life?' the reply of Jesus concerns itself instead with the Kingdom of God (Mk. 10.17).

Such life is wholly derived from Christ. It is pre-eminently present in Christ himself: 'In him was life' (Jn. 1.4, 5.26). Christ imparts it to those who believe in him (Jn. 3.16, 6.47) and hear his words (5.24, 6.63). Christ is life itself, the Bread of life, the Resurrection and the Life. He that has the Son had life (1 Jn. 5.12). Those who are brought within the orbit of the kingdom find through Christ this new quality of authentic inner life.

In some respects this is a useful synonym for the kingdom, but it relates only to one element in the kingdom. It is incomplete and unless supplemented by other emphases it may lead to a one-sided, unbalanced, and even misleading, understanding of the kingdom. For instance, its emphasis is only on the individual experience, and omits the strong element of moral and social content which both Matthew and Paul seek to preserve by their emphasis on righteousness. At the same time it does emphasise one genuine element in the kingdom (and one perhaps that some Christians did less than justice to). Where God through Christ is given the supreme place in a human life, the inner quality of that life is transformed into something wonderful. This quality of life moreover is such that even death itself will not destroy it. This is because it is derived from God and is the result of union with God. God is its eternal source and Christ its God-given mediator.

When, however, this element in the kingdom is isolated and treated as complete in itself, it leads to distortion. This distortion is found in some of Paul's opponents who delighted in the spiritual and emotional privileges of this life available in the Kingdom of God, but paid little heed to the standards of conduct which obedience to the will of god imposed, and made light of the moral responsibilities involved. So Paul had to remind them often, as in Colossians 3.1–15, that if they are 'risen into new life with Christ' and delight in Christ as their 'life', this involves not only discarding the blatant sins of the body, but also the more subtle sins of the disposition, and further, not only avoiding evil things but, more positively, allowing the moral qualities of Christ himself to assert themselves as part of this new life.

'Life' therefore is a valid equivalent of some elements in the kingdom, but needs to be supplemented by other words if it is to be an adequate representation of all that the kingdom involves.

3. The Holy Spirit

We have noticed that in both Acts and the Pauline letters there is a considerable reduction in the number of times the Kingdom of God is mentioned as compared with the synoptic gospels, and a great increase in the frequency of the references to the Holy Spirit. Many of the functions ascribed to the Holy Spirit in these books correspond closely to the functions of the kingdom in the synoptics, so that the two may be regarded as in some ways parallel. Moreover the two concepts sometimes are brought into close association. Indeed this is true even in the synoptics. In Mt. 12.28, for instance, Jesus is reported as saying: 'If I by the Spirit of God cast out demons, the Kingdom of God has burst in upon you'. One cannot be sure that this association of the Spirit and the kingdom goes back to Jesus, but certainly Matthew felt it appropriate to use the words in this close relationship.

Perhaps we should not press for any special significance in the fact that Mark places the first announcement of the proclamation of Jesus: 'The Kingdom of God is at hand' in the verse which immediately follows those which tell how the Holy Spirit entered into Jesus on the occasion of his baptism, and then drove him out into the lonely places to face Satan's temptation. Nor can we press the significance, in relation to the kingdom, of Lk. 4.18 where Jesus is described as visiting his own town of Nazareth, and reading in the synagogue the opening words of Isaiah 61: 'The Spirit of the Lord is upon me . . .', concluding with his own application of the passage to his hearers: 'Today has this scripture been fulfilled in your ears'. But it does indicate that for Luke the possession of the Spirit was the source of the authority behind the proclamation and ministry of Jesus.

More important, though still somewhat ambiguous in its significance, is the intriguing variation which is found in some manuscripts of Lk. 11.2, where the petition (in the Lord's Prayer), 'Your Kingdom come' is replaced by the words: 'Let your Holy Spirit come upon us and cleanse us'. It would be difficult to make out a case for regarding these words as coming originally from Luke, since the more reliable manuscripts do not contain them, but the reading does show that some among the early Christians must have regarded this wording of the clause in the prayer as not only roughly equivalent to the more conventional alternative, but probably more intelligible to the readers they had in mind.

The association of these two ideas appears again in Jn. 3.5 where those who are to enter the Kingdom of God must first be 'born of the Spirit'. Also at Rom. 14.7 the Kingdom of God is described as consisting of righteousness, peace and joy *in the Holy Spirit*. Here, as in Mt. 12.28, the activity of the Spirit is the agent of the kingdom. Moreover there is a close parallel between this verse in Romans which ascribes righteousness, peace and joy to the kingdom and Gal. 5.22 where love, joy and peace are attributed to the Holy Spirit. But in many other passages also Paul ascribes to the work of the Holy Spirit the same kind of good things which Jesus saw as the marks of the presence of the kingdom—such things as righteousness, salvation, life, peace and joy. The Holy Spirit for Paul, as the Kingdom for Jesus, is a gift to be received from God by faith and having been received to be allowed to rule and shape the believer's life and actions. The same is true in Acts: both the kingdom and the Holy Spirit convey the message of God's gift to the believer of power, healing and salvation.

As time passed and the Christian Church worked mainly among non-Jewish populations, the Spirit came to have many advantages over the Kingdom of God as an effective means of offering the gospel. In Greek, as in English, it is almost impossible to divest the word 'kingdom' of ideas of space and locality and immobility, and to represent it, as it was for Jesus, as a vigorous, mobile, spiritual force. It is hard also to adjust one's mind so as to think of the kingdom as in fact the ruling presence of a *Person*, wholly personal in his dealings with man. The Spirit of God did not suffer from these disabilities.

The traditional phrase, 'the Kingdom of God', was so firmly enshrined in the memory of the original proclamation of Jesus that it continued to be used as a kind of standard of reference, yet increasingly it was found that the Holy Spirit served more effectively the cause of evangelism and pastoral care.

4. The Kingdom of Christ

An increasing tendency among New Testament writers was to speak of the Kingdom of God as the Kingdom of Christ. It is true that only once is the phrase 'my Kingdom' placed on the lips of Jesus himself. This is at Lk. 22.29 where Jesus promises his disciples that they will 'eat and drink at my table in my Kingdom'. It would be difficult to argue that these represent the exact words of Jesus. In Mk. 14.25 and Mt. 26.29 Jesus speaks of drinking wine 'new' *in the Kingdom of God*. It seems more likely that here Luke allowed what to him had become an appropriate mode of speech to be read back into the ministry of Jesus. Certainly Luke places similar utterances on the lips of people other than Jesus in his gospel. For instance, at Lk. 23.42, the dying thief asks Jesus to remember him 'when you come into your Kingdom'; and earlier, at 1.33, the angels promise to Mary of her son-to-be that 'of his Kingdom there shall be no end'.

There is only one verse in the fourth gospel which speaks of the Kingdom as Christ's. It is Jn. 18.36; but in this one verse Jesus is represented as speaking no less than three times the phrase 'my Kingdom': 'My Kingdom is not of this world . . . else my servants would fight'. In Acts the precise phrase 'Kingdom of Christ' does not occur, but in two passages Christ and the kingdom are placed in very close association almost as parallel expressions. At Acts 8.12 Philip's preaching is 'about the Kingdom of God and the name of Christ'; and at Acts 28.31 (the last verse in Acts) Paul is described as continuing to 'preach the Kingdom of God and teach about the Lord Jesus Christ'. There are, however, precise references to Christ and his Kingdom in the Pauline (or post-Pauline) writings: 'God has transferred us into the kingdom of his beloved Son' (Col. 1.13), and similar references occur in Eph. 5.5, 2 Tim. 4.1, 4.18. There is one also at 2 Peter 1.11.

In 1 Cor. 15.24 Paul speaks of Christ handing over 'the Kingdom' to God. Certainly this does not speak of the kingdom as Christ's, and seems to envisage the future in somewhat different terms from the famous words of Rev. 11.15 which declare: 'The Kingdom of the world has become the Kingdom of the Lord and of his Christ, and he will reign for ever and ever'. This suggests that for the writer of Revelation Christ's kingdom is to be an everlasting kingdom (as Luke 1.33 also expected)—perhaps entirely equated with the Kingdom of God. For Paul, however, Christ's work was to make a vital contribution to the eternal Kingdom of God, and after that God would be all in all.

It is unlikely that Jesus himself ever spoke of the kingdom as his kingdom. His message concerned the Kingdom of God, a kingdom whose reality and whose victories were evidenced in the ministry of Jesus, who was God's servant endowed with God's Spirit and entrusted with God's purposes. But Christian believers became more and more certain that Jesus was not just one servant of God among others, but one so uniquely the servant of God that he totally represented God to them. What Christ was, was seen to be a revelation and interpretation of God himself. Everything that could be said of God could be said of Christ—at least so far as this world and God's presence and activity in the world was concerned.

This way of thinking of Christ was the more important because in fact the word 'God' by itself was an indeterminate word. One could not be sure what any one speaker meant by it. It had to be shared for instance with the Jews; and indeed not only with Jews, but with pagan Greeks, whose thoughts of God were not Christian thoughts. For Christians what had been actually seen and heard in Jesus Christ defined what could be regarded as Christian truth about God, for the Christian God was best understood as the God who was in Christ.

It became easy, therefore, for Christians to think of the kingdom of God as it was known and active in Christ's ministry and in the life of the growing Church as the Kingdom of Christ. As such it had indeed more precise character than the vaguer term 'the Kingdom of God'. Paul in 1 Cor. 15.24 seems to suggest that the Kingdom of Christ could be thought of as the rule which Christ has inaugurated here on earth for God and which he will hand over to God after the Parousia and 'the end'. What we may think of as God's Kingdom established in human hearts and human society is for Paul the kingdom which Christ will hand over to his

Father. Perhaps therefore, following Paul, we may think of Christ's Kingdom as a kingdom with reality and significance so long as human history lasts, but destined in God's good time to be taken up into the larger, unending Kingdom of God.

9. CONCLUSIONS AND MODERN APPLICATIONS

Jesus and the Kingdom

One of the most striking characteristics of Jesus was that he made God real to his fellow men. Moreover God, as he became real through Jesus, was strikingly different from the God of conventional religion. This meant that the teaching of Jesus about God often roused in people shocked surprise. Sometimes this turned into hostility. Sometimes it awakened new insights and called forth enthusiastic and wholehearted —if sometimes bewildered—devotion.

The essence of his message was that God was not aloof, distant or offended, but one who, as friend and deliverer of men and women, was actively present in his world, one who was even now initiating a vigorous campaign to set men free from the evil forces which oppressed them. God was coming to re-claim his own people. They had to be re-claimed because forces hostile to God—and therefore hostile to human life —had subdued them and brought them under the domination of Satan, God's enemy. Satan indeed was now the factual ruler of this present world, and evil spirits, the agents of his rule, tyrannised over men and women. God's immediate coming in power meant that the reign of these evil powers was threatened and doomed. In their place God's reign—his kingdom—was to be established, and as that reign spread its authority many who now felt themselves helpless before the powers of evil would experience joyful deliverance and salvation.

This coming of God in power to rescue his people from this enslavement to an alien power was proclaimed as good news or the gospel—the Gospel of the Kingdom of God. It was good news because it brought the news that one stronger than their present oppressors was near at hand to set men free.

This message of deliverance for captives carried with it a rallying call to all men, to join forces with the one who was bringing deliverance. If God's reign was to prevail, going from strength to strength, those who had been set free must themselves become loyal and active subjects of the new ruler. Only so could the new joy of freedom be sustained. It was not enough merely to expect God to set men free from oppressors whom they hated. God's purpose also was to set men free from all that hindered men from serving him with glad and free commitment. He needed men and women as his allies and servants who besides being themselves delivered would be wholly committed to him, and in their total obedience to him willing to sacrifice anything which disputed God's complete control of their lives. But to those who both welcomed God's coming as a deliverer and also yielded themselves to him as servant of his further purposes, God gave the great privilege of true life, life as God had meant it to be, fullness of life, eternal life.

God's coming, then as always, was a disturbing mixture of these two contrasting features. On the one hand there was the promise, the offer, the gift, just to be received for the taking. On the other hand there was the demand, the requirement following the offered gift. At best, the experience of God's goodness, freely offered to men in the experience of deliverance, led men in gratitude to total commitment to his cause; and in such cases total commitment opened the way to the discovery of even deeper joys and more lasting happiness than had previously been guessed at. The proclamation of these two complementary truths was embodied by Jesus in the watchword: 'The reign (kingdom) of God is here', a rallying call which both offered hope and claimed authority.

In this coming rule of God, offer and demand are interlocked. The coming of the kingdom into human life offers the joys of deliverance—freedom, peace, life, salvation. But the teaching of Jesus about the kingdom includes also firm emphasis on the need for obedience to the new ruler, and the cost which may be involved in offering that complete obedience—the cost of sacrificing not only evil things which defy God but also good things, if they resist or dispute God's authority. The facing of this cost and the hard choices it presents confronts would-be disciples with painful moments of decision. But God's gifts for men are not forced on to reluctant people; they must be freely accepted. If, however, we accept God's gifts, it is not just his gifts which we take; we are in effect accepting God himself. And to accept God into our lives means accepting him both as he offers gifts and demands obedience. It means learning how to wait in order to receive strength (Is. 40.31) or 'power from on high' (Lk. 24.49) and also 'how to rise up and follow'. Both these responses to God are included in the word 'faith' on which Jesus laid such great emphasis.

The message of the kingdom, therefore, is a balanced blend of gift and command. The most immediate and obvious emphasis, however, since it is implicit in the name itself, is on God's right to rule and on the total obedience required of those who enrol as subjects in his kingdom (or, to put it another way, enlist on active service in his army). This is assumed in all teaching about the kingdom. But the privileges of the kingdom also are immense. When God is accepted as ruler, his power can tame and expel evil powers which otherwise could cripple and torment human life and destroy human happiness. He can set men free from such evil things as emotional disturbances which not only drain all happiness out of life, but may also induce what appear as physical illnesses as well. He can set men free from the tyranny of appetite, of fear and anxiety and the foolish hankering after money and social status. Release *from* these tyrants can free us *for* life's true joy.

For Jesus the word 'Father' indicated far better than 'King' the quality of the relationship between the ruler and his subjects, but whether God is thought of as King or Father, there are the implications of a community of those who acknowledge his authority. Right relationship with the Father create and maintain right relationships within the rest of the family. The words of Jesus, both about the kingdom and elsewhere, show that for him this family was open to people of all nations and cultures. It was equally open to people of all social classes, whether religious or irreligious (not excluding taxgatherers and sinners, the most disreputable ranks of Jewish society), and even to little children.

The essence of the message of Jesus was that God in his kingly power was about to take charge of his harassed people and set them free from all the hostile domination of evil. But what was beginning in Galilee was only a tiny seed from which vast results would grow. God's rule, now showing its first signs of success, would in due course and before long, come in power. What was now incipient would become dominant. Those who died before this was achieved were, however, not lost to God's Kingdom. They would be welcomed into that sphere of the kingdom which was eternal, beyond this earthly existence, there to share in joyous celebration in the presence of God. It was the life of that eternal kingdom which in the ministry of Jesus was breaking through into the world of time and space. The time was coming when what God was now beginning would embrace all mankind in complete triumph, when what was God's by right would become God's in fact. That was part of God's future. It was this for which his followers would live and hope and strive.

What Jesus proclaimed about the Kingdom of God is not to be thought of as just a short-term policy, applicable only to the limited period of the earthly ministry of Jesus. It was not something which was terminated by his death. His resurrection, which revitalised his disconsolate followers, had the effect of making them realise that all that Jesus had stood for and died for was not just an ephemeral nine-days' wonder belonging to the past, but the beginning of a new age, a continuing truth about God and his people.

The New Testament Interpreters of the Kingdom

As the Gospel of Jesus went out into the non-Jewish world, it was found that his message about the 'Kingdom of God' needed to be interpreted, either by adding explanatory words (such as 'righteousness' or 'life') or by substituting a more readily intelligible alternative (such as Holy Spirit or Christ himself). 'Life' indicated the rich quality of inward experience created by the presence of the kingdom. 'Righteousness' ensured that the qualities of integrity, uprightness and love for others which the kingdom brought were not overlooked. The Holy Spirit vividly represented the liveliness and vitality of God's presence in human life. To speak of Christ as the bearer of the kingdom and the kingdom as Christ's rule in human life and society gives to the kingdom its own special Christian character in moral and spiritual terms.

Modern Interpretations of the Kingdom of God

Some may question whether it is sufficient today merely to interpret the meaning of the Kingdom of God by adding explanatory phrases to it in order to emphasise important aspects of it which otherwise might be overlooked. Is the Kingdom of God itself any longer an effective symbol? Cannot the same essential truth which it once conveyed effectively in the ministry of Jesus be better conveyed today in entirely different words? If so, should we hesitate to use these alternatives merely because they are different from the time-honoured phrase? It is the spiritual truth by which men's lives can be transformed that really matters, not the particular words in which that truth is expressed. The kingdom is not a 'thing' or an 'entity'; it is a relationship between God and his people, between God and his world. Where God is welcomed, obeyed and rejoiced in, there is the Kingdom of God. It may be that, with us as with Paul, the Kingdom of God will no longer seem to be the most appropriate vehicle for proclaiming the meaning of the gospel. For us it is rather a symbol of the message proclaimed by and embodied in Jesus. As such it remains as a kind of recognised standard of truth and goodness to which we can appeal in order to check and correct tendencies and enthusiasms of the present time. We must continually ask of any new expression of Christian truth whether it tallies with what Jesus announced in terms of the kingdom, but we need not feel tied to the phrase itself.

If today we wish to make real the truth that God is restlessly seeking to gain entrance into human lives to transform them inwardly, we may well be guided by the early interpreters and prefer to use the concept of the Spirit of God.

Conventional Christianity has always been a little uneasy about the Holy Spirit and has often sought to confine his boundless energy within such recognised channels as baptism, Holy Communion, ordination, etc.—that which the Church can authorise and dispense. We tend to feel uncomfortable when people speak of God's Spirit sweeping people off their feet, directing their lives into entirely new courses, filling them with joyful exuberance. Yet it must have seemed very much like that when the Kingdom of God through Jesus claimed the lives of the first disciples.

The modern Pentecostal movements are a vivid reminder of this Christian truth which has down the centuries been often feared, and in consequence avoided and neglected, in the established churches. The special emphasis of such movements is on the truth that God in his Holy Spirit is eager to break into human lives and cleanse, renew and empower them. This is a New Testament truth which all Christians need to lay hold of. The great danger of the Pentecostal movements, however, is that this one aspect of truth is stressed to the exclusion or belittlement of other elements of Christian truth. For instance, the coming of the Spirit is sometimes represented in terms of emotional ecstasy, with its chief expression as the gift of speaking in tongues which this brings. In the New Testament, however, this gift receives nothing like the same degree of emphasis as the Christlike qualities of character which the Holy Spirit forms within the Christian, what in such a passage as Galatians 5 are called 'the fruit of the Spirit'. The Pentecostalists are, however, doing us all the service of reminding us of this forgotten New Testament truth that God in his Holy Spirit is seeking to gain entrance to human lives, so as to fill them with his benefits and bring them into total obedience to his will—what Jesus meant when he proclaimed the coming of the Kingdom of God. But by itself this can all too easily become an unbalanced presentation of the message of Jesus, unless closely co-ordinated into it is an equal emphasis on righteousness and Jesus as Lord.

Similarly God's Kingdom brought great 'blessedness' to those who received it. God's coming into life to rule and control it produces new qualities of inner unity and happiness.

In the New Testament this is often spoken of as 'life', and this same word is one which is equally current in modern thought. God's coming into human life to rule it brings to us true life, life at its best, authentic life, life as God meant it to be. If this new life is seen in sharp contrast to the frustration, 'alienation', defeat and misery which preceded it, then the emphasis may be placed in what we have been rescued from or saved from. In that case words like 'deliverance' and 'salvation' may still have their appropriateness. But 'life' may have certain advantages, since it carries a more positive sound and has, for many, a less sanctimonious flavour. It serves to emphasise the Christian truth that the rule of God, when accepted into human life, is not an irksome, restrictive irritation, but a liberating and fulfilling relationship, which makes people want to say: 'This is what life was meant to be'.

Paul used the phrase 'the Kingdom of God' in order to appeal to a venerated standard of the past, to remind people who had become Christians that what was right and fair and good must take first place in their lives. These very words are the ones by which we can still describe God's will for human life. Righteousness today may seem too pompous a word to make a wide appeal. Indeed any explicit appeal to moral values is apt to expose the speaker in today's atmosphere to the taunt of being a prig. But everyone has some sense of what is right, even when we do not practise it ourselves. We often hear people say indignantly: 'It's not right'. And even those who demand permissiveness in all areas of what we call private morality can wax very indignant about conditions in society which are not right. The Christian will want to make right or righteousness his aim, but he will want his sense of what is right to be shaped by what God has revealed through Christ. He will also insist that it applies to personal conduct no less than to social issues, and that acknowledging it without practising it is a kind of dishonesty.

What is 'right', however, forces us into the context of social morality, because what is right has a direct bearing not only on individuals but on communities. Indeed right is preeminently a social concept. True righteousness means being 'right with God', and this in turn means acting right by our fellow men. The Christian understanding of righteousness is not just not doing wrong but positively doing right, which leads to love for neighbour—and for stranger, and even for enemy. This is the fulfilling of God's law (Rom. 13.10). And love, even more than righteousness, is a community word. It means that the Christian wishes for all men the privileges and opportunities he wants for himself and his loved ones. To love God and to love one's neighbour is that which gives direction to life for every Christian. Righteousness interpreted through love is a modern equivalent of the Kingdom of God.

This moral aspect of the Kingdom of God, with an emphasis on its corporate and social implications, is the one which has received most emphasis in this century, perhaps because in earlier centuries it was the aspect most neglected. When it is stressed to the exclusion of other elements in the kingdom, it presents a one-sided and unbalanced picture. It is, however, one genuine part of the message of the kingdom. Such a presentation of the kingdom is to be found, for instance, among Christian socialists whose aim is to establish the Kingdom of God on earth and who interpret it in the following terms:

(i) It will be a selfless society in contrast to the present society organised to encourage greed and self-interest.

(ii) It will have no separatism—no racialism, no nationalism, no class consciousness.

(iii) It will value qualities which further better human relationships more than mere raising of material standards of living.

(iv) Beyond mere legal justice it will administer society with love, compassion and understanding.

This represents an ideal of the kingdom translated into society. It is a worthy aim. But much more than human endeavour will be needed to make such an ideal into a reality. The Kingdom of God begins by God's action in individual lives, in the creation of good men. And good men are the only sure basis for a good society.

In recent years Christians have become concerned not only

to establish a 'righteous society' within their own national boundaries, but to remove 'what is wrong' wherever in the world it is found. World hunger, lack of medical care, the homelessness of refugees, racial oppression, wherever they occur, are seen as evils which need to be put right. A concern for God's righteousness, God's Kingdom, will include a restless, passionate concern to bring relief to all who suffer under such removable injustices and deprivations in any part of the world.

This concern is relatively easy for those who live in democratic countries where the right to advocate methods for the removal of injustices is recognised. Those Christians, however, who live under dictatorships are in a much more difficult situation. For them open protest is forbidden and punishable by imprisonment or death. All peaceful methods of removing injustice have been made illegal. For many sincere Christians in such conditions revolution, even involving violence, seems the only way left for removing unbearable wrongs. Their revolutionary theology sees in the Kingdom of God a summons to establish righteousness and justice, even if it means both facing and inflicting death. Other Christians fear that violence in the end creates more problems than it solves, and insist that violence has no part in the Kingdom of God and of Christ. Christians are therefore divided in their judgement whether the righteousness inherent in the Kingdom of God can ever be furthered by violent action. But though the methods to be used are not agreed, there can be no doubt that all who are concerned to see the Kingdom of God on earth will be passionately eager to see righteousness (including both personal and civil 'rights') established not only in their own land but throughout the world, and will not shrink from effective action to achieve it, even where it is costly and painful.

We noted earlier how among the interpreters of the kingdom within the New Testament there was a strong tendency to associate the kingdom very closely with Christ himself.

Jesus himself was in part responsible for this. He spoke of God's saving power, operating through his own ministry to heal the mentally and emotionally distressed, as evidence of the presence of the kingdom (Mt. 11.28). Other New Testament writers speak of the Kingdom of Christ without distinguishing it from the Kingdom of God. Marcion in the second century summed it up in the aphorism that for Christians Christ himself is the Kingdom of God. A little later Origen called Jesus *autobasileia*, the very kingdom itself. This approach has much to commend it for people today. The word kingdom has an antiquated sound, and its meaning is perhaps best represented by the acknowledgement of Christ as Lord. 'Jesus is Lord' is said to be the earliest and simplest form of Christian creed. To accept Jesus as Lord is the same as to receive or to enter the Kingdom of God, because for the Christian Jesus represents the rule of God in human life. To discover him as Saviour is to find him the one who can still cast out demons and rescue from the power of evil, controlling wayward passions and appetites, melting bitterness, jealousy, resentment, hate and greed out of the human heart; he is the one who can enrich the human heart with life, abundant life, the life found in the Kingdom of God. Obedience to his words about loving one's neighbour as oneself, even loving strangers and enemies, about doing to others what we should like them to do to us, is as near as any rule of thumb can be to indicating what is right. Nor is it just a matter of obeying his recorded words. He is also a living personal presence in our lives with whom we can consult on all matters of conduct. Paul let us into the secret of his own innermost ambition: it was 'to gain the approval of Jesus Christ' (2 Cor. 5.9). What Jesus Christ approves is what is right. He was for Paul the new law of God (Gal. 6.2), and Paul who no longer recognised the Mosaic law gladly acknowledged that he was still under one law—'the law of Christ' (1 Cor. 9.21). Jesus Christ, however, not only embodies all that we mean by right, but he also is one who can bring enabling power by which frail human beings can alone hope to do the right. The living Christ, like the vitalising Spirit of God, can bring a new quality of inward life to the committed Christian. Indeed it becomes almost impossible to separate in experience what is meant by the living Christ and the Holy Spirit. Paul indeed speaks of Christ as a 'life-giving Spirit' (1 Cor. 15.45).

The early Christians prayed: 'Come, Lord Jesus' (Rev. 22.20; or used the Aramaic words as preserved at 1 Cor. 16.21). Sometimes this was prayed as people met in fellowship, perhaps in celebration of the sacrament of Holy Communion. It was then a prayer that Christ would come in his spiritual presence to renew and sustain the individual Christian and the society of Christians. It was also a prayer for the final victory of Christ, when it was believed he would come again in power and great glory and all enemies would be defeated, a time when evil would be destroyed and righteousness would prevail for ever, when 'at the name of Jesus every knee shall bow, in heaven and on earth and under the earth, and every tongue confess that Jesus Christ is Lord to the glory of God the Father' (Phil. 2.10,11).

So Christians have also prayed; 'Your Kingdom come', and its meaning is not dissimilar from 'Come, Lord Jesus'. This is a prayer that God will here and now take charge of our wilful, disobedient world, that he will establish his will in our lives, in the lives of our fellow Christians and our Christian community, in the life of society as a whole and of the entire world. It is a prayer that God will drive out evil things that oppose him and oppress and degrade human life, evil things which human life on its own seems both unwilling and unable to resist, or finds itself harassed and discouraged in the weary struggle against them. In this prayer we look to God to bring his salvation from threatening evil with the gift of peace and joy and fulness of life in place of stress and strain. We pray that with these great privileges God will bring our lives into total obedience to him—in our personal behaviour, even in our thinking and feeling, in our social conduct, in the way we think of others and the way we treat them, that we may learn to love all men and seek their welfare as our own. Since today we are privileged in Britain to live as responsible citizens in a democratic country, where our voice may be heard and our vote counted, our prayer is for God's rule to shape our country's laws and customs and our whole standards of social behaviour; and we commit ourselves in the prayer to seek God's righteousness in the exercise of our citizenship. We are citizens also, though in a less direct sense, of the world. We pray that God's righteous rule will prevail in every grouping of nations— the European Common Market, the Commonwealth, in the countries of Asia and Africa and the Americas, the United Nations—and throughout the world, and we will think and work as well as pray that this shall be so. It is true that we as human beings cannot establish God's Kingdom by merely human endeavours. Yet the kingdom cannot come to nations unless it first wins great victories in individual lives. As we pray for the coming of God's Kingdom, common honesty demands that we pray first for that kingdom to be established within our own lives, because that is the area where we have most choice and influence; and when something of the kingdom has come there, we shall give our best endeavours to spread the spirit of that kingdom into every area of life which our influence touches, personal relationships, social life, national politics, international relationships and world need. All this is what our prayer means.

When we pray for God's Kingdom to come, it does not mean that we desire or expect some supernatural, apocalyptic event coinciding with the end of the world. Our prayer (in Matthew's wording of it) is that God's Kingdom will come *on earth* as it is in heaven, that, as God rules and receives perfect obedience in heaven, so he shall come to rule on earth. We recognise that the word 'kingdom' sounds old-fashioned and in need of interpretation. Our prayer for its coming may sound more intelligible to many if we analyse it as a prayer for God's righteousness to prevail, for God' Spirit to bring the enabling power, for God's people to receive the privilege of true life. Perhaps too it is more meaningful if we pray for it as Christ's Kingdom, since to call it Christ's defines its character and quality. But when we have identified the constituent elements in God's Kingdom, we still need one comprehensive term to embrace them all and hold them all in proper balance, so that no one element will dominate to the exclusion of others. So we return gratefully to the original term 'The Kingdom of God', preferring that even to 'the Kingdom of Christ'. Christ, it is true, is the mediator of that kingdom, God's agent in its coming. But its origin and destiny lie within the eternal purposes of God.

So the phrase 'The Kingdom of God' though not expressed in twentieth-century idiom, bears special authority still for Christians because of the central place it held in the teaching of Jesus, and even today remains effective as the one adequate comprehensive term for holding together in unity all the separable elements which constitute it. So we still pray 'Your Kingdom come', a very relevant prayer both for our present task of joyous obedience to God's will and for our future and confident hope that the time will come when

> The kingdom of this world has become the Kingdom of our lord and of his Christ,
> And he shall reign for ever and ever (Rev. 11.15).

SELECT BIBLIOGRAPHY

Bultmann, R., *History of the Synoptic Tradition* (Blackwell, 1963).
Bundy, W. E., *Jesus and the First Three Gospels* (Harvard U.P., 1955).
Caird, G. B., *St. Luke* (Pelican, 1963).
Davies, J. G., *Christians, Politics and Violent Revolution* (S.C.M., 1976).
Dodd, C. H., *Parables of the Kingdom* (Nisbet, 1935).
Dunn, J. D. G., *Jesus and the Spirit* (S.C.M., 1975).
Glasson, T. F., *Second Advent* (Epworth, 1945).
Harnack, A., *What is Christianity?* (Williams and Norgate, 1901).
Jeremias, J., *Parables of Jesus* (S.C.M., 1954).
—— *New Testament Theology* (S.C.M., 1971).
Käsemann, E., *New Testament Questions of Today* (S.C.M., 1969).
Kümmel, E. G., *Promise and Fulfilment* (S.C.M., 1956).
Linnemann, E., *Parables of Jesus* (S.P.C.K., 1966).
Manson, T. W., *Sayings of Jesus* (S.C.M., 1937).
Mitton, C. L., *Jesus: The Fact behind the Faith* (Mowbrays, 1975).
Neill, S., *Interpretation of the New Testament* (Oxford U.P., 1964).
Perrin, N., *Kingdom of God in Teaching of Jesus* (S.C.M., 1963).
—— *Jesus and the Language of the Kingdom* (S.C.M., 1975).
Robinson, J. A. T., *Jesus and His Coming* (S.C.M., 1957).
Schmithals, W., *Apocalyptic Movement* (Abingdon, 1975).
Schweitzer, A., *Quest of Historical Jesus* (A. and C. Black, 1910).
Temple, W., *Christianity and Social Order* (Penguin, 1972, S.P.C.K., 1976).
Vermes, G., *Jesus the Jew* (Collins, 1973).
Weiss, J., *Earliest Christianity* (Harper, 1959).

Abbreviations (referring to Translation of the Bible)

A.V.   Authorised Version.
L.B.   Living Bible.
N.E.B. New English Bible.
R.S.V. Revised Standard Version.
T.E.V. Today's English Version (or Bible for Today).